THE MAN AND A BOY

Teach Me to Be

Dialogues between Jesus and an Abused Boy

James J. McBride, PhD

iUniverse, Inc.

New York   Bloomington

The Man and a Boy

Teach Me to Be

iUniverse books may be ordered through booksellers or by contacting:

iUniverse
1663 Liberty Drive
Bloomington, IN 47403
www.iuniverse.com
1-800-Authors (1-800-288-4677)

ISBN: 978-1-4401-2678-9 (pbk)
ISBN: 978-1-4401-2680-2(cloth)
ISBN: 978-1-4401-2679-6 (ebk)

Library of Congress Control Number: 2009924011

Printed in the United States of America

iUniverse rev. date: 5/12/2009

To my wife, Janet, who knows me as husband,
loves me as a friend and companion

To my children, who know me as Dad

To my grandchildren, who know me as Papa

To my great-grandchildren, who may learn from me

To Nanny Janet, who has two names for me:

McClownee the Humble Clown
and
Mick the Astronomer

Contents

About the Author

Teach me to be! This is the author's mantra. From the state of a young boy to the stage of an aged man, he cried out seeking *nurture …* "To be or not to be." He knew, intuitively, in his heart, that he needed others to teach him how to achieve so he could teach others in return.

Dr. James J. McBride retired in 1996 from his teaching profession of almost forty years, a time of joy mixed with sadness. The *joy* came with people eulogizing his achievements; the *sadness* came with his understanding that achievements are fleeting.

The author was one of two teachers to work as a team teaching Russian teachers. He returned from Vladivostok, Russia, in January 1995, after spending many weeks teaching Russian teachers how to recover from the wreckage of a command economy in Russia and establish an environment in which a new Russia, based on free markets and democracy, might grow. The U.S. State Department and the New Russian Ministry of Education believed that two American teachers could possibly affect changes that might influence Russian thoughts about the free market. American instructors guiding Russian teachers to understand and teach American economics was a small beginning in resolving a huge problem.

Dr. McBride has taught physics, astronomy, math, biology, psychology, electronics, economics, history, and government. The City of Coronado, California, and the County of San Diego, California, proclaimed May 7, 1992, as Dr. James J. McBride Day. San Diego City, County, and the State of California honored Dr. McBride as the 1992 State Economics Teacher of the Year. The San Diego County Service Center Council presented Dr. James J. McBride with the 1995 California Teachers Association "WHO" (We Honor Ours) Award.

He received his Doctor of Philosophy in Leadership and Human

Behavior in 1975. He completed studies for clinical psychology in 1977. He received the honor and a monetary stipend from the State of California for being a Master Teacher from 1971 to 1973.

He received his Master of Science in Physics Education in 1965. His master's degree was the result of many National Science Foundation (NSF) grants and stipends in mathematics and physics. Other achievements go back a decade.

All too quickly, after retiring, the joy of his achievements was short-lived. In his search for a new achievement that would satisfy his compulsion to teach, he opened a door to an awe-inspiring roomful of knowledge, understanding, and wisdom. It is his private room of thoughts and ideas. From this private room, he will teach others through a series of discussions between the personas of his personality: McClownee the Humble Clown, and Mick the Astronomer.

Dr. McBride wants students to enter the open door of his private room, where his two personas, McClownee and Mick, converse and discuss all that he ever learned "to be." McClownee is the left half of his fashioned persona. Mick is the right side of his Irish-fashioned persona. Dr. McBride's wife, Janet (she is called Mom by some, and Nanny by others) gave him these names of personas to remind him to live his life as a humble clown and as Mickey, a mixture of many ethnic groups. He is a mongrel.

McClownee is Dr. McBride's presentation to his world. Janet set out his clothes each day and made sure he was a fashion plate as a teacher. She made sure he was always stylish. Her value system rubbed off on him. Her passionate chastity, her sense of right and wrong, her love of beauty, and her ability as an artistic designer of their home made McClownee a real persona of Dr. McBride's personality.

McClownee exists in reality as an eight-inch figurine clown doll. He sits on the desk, a reminder to Dr. McBride that his life illustrates a humble, happy, styling, outward appearance. He realizes he is a picture of Janet's creation. However, Janet is the frame that surrounds her creation to the world. McClownee is the contrast of what you see on the outside, which can be so different from what is on the inside of his persona. McClownee is to remind Dr. McBride that the ultimate achievement is to seek enlightenment. McClownee is a symbol of the difference between love and hate, the difference between compassionate kindness and violent abuse. McClownee represents Dr. McBride's values, feelings, and emotions—his sense of happiness and sadness in his everyday experiences.

Mickey also sits in Dr. McBride's office as a bear replica of Albert Einstein. His son Chris gave the Albert Einstein bear to him when he taught about the universe in the Southwestern Junior College Planetarium. Chris wrote a paper for Dr. McBride's astronomy class, comparing Dr. McBride to Albert Einstein. He got an A for the course. The bear became more than a replica of Albert Einstein. It joined the three figurines of Mickey as the Sorcerer's Apprentice: an eclectic symbol unifying the sciences. Dr. McBride's enlightenment as "Mick" was a mixture of math and many sciences.

Mick's achievement at enlightenment is to demonstrate the awe-inspiring works of the universe. *Mickey* represents scientists trying to understand the awesome energies of the universe, the intricacies of DNA and genetics, and the frightening knowledge of chaos theory.

McClownee and Mickey represent Dr. McBride's values, logic, and reasoning, and his empirical sense of gaining knowledge. The Dialogues will be the written discussions between McClownee and Mickey. McClownee and Mickey have discussions going all the time in Dr. McBride's awareness. The two of them converse during Dr. McBride's every waking moment. They will put their discussions and feelings into this book.

However, they decided that Jesus was the greatest teacher. Therefore, they present their Dialogues with a modern Jesus, "The Man," being challenged to teach a young boy how to overcome his abuse by gaining self-respect and self-esteem, the heart of being human.

McClownee and Mickey's Dialogues will illustrate the determination of the boy as he seeks to learn what he values. He will experience working hard to learn the many languages that human beings possess. He learns the value of hard work as he seeks enlightenment through the concepts of time, the laws of science, the moral laws, and the language of mathematics.

McClownee and Mickey's Dialogues' focus is for the boy to gain knowledge about the creation, understanding that knowledge leads to a Creator—and that the Creator wants a connection with the creation, based on wisdom and unconditional love. A final riddle explains it all. The book thus gets its title: *The Man and a* boy. The subtitle, *Teach Me to Be: Dialogues between Jesus and an Abused Boy*, amplifies the title.

This book is a tribute to honor his rock-solid wife, Janet. The book's contents, and especially the conclusions of the last four Dialogues, are a compliment to her life. She wrote a summary of an abused boy meeting The Man who helps him overcome the violent abuse from his biological father. At the time, this clarified Dr. McBride's thinking.

When he doubted retiring, Janet was the one constant in his life that he loved more than life itself. From the moment he decided to retire, he devoted the rest of his moments to her. She received his unconditional love. His achievements would allow him to learn and teach about unconditional love.

Author's Note

Teach me to be! My mantra cries out to be nurtured by one more achievement. I want to write a book as a legacy for my family, friends, and all those people who have been or are being abused in myriad ways.

This book, *The Man and a Boy*, created by *McClownee* the Humble Clown and *Mick* the Astronomer, has been a feather in my mind for a lifetime. Most of the time, the feather just floated around. During those flashes when I learned something new, the feather would tickle the left side of my mind, the McClownee persona, or the right side of my mind, the Mick persona.

Awareness started with my instructions for baptism, as I was a convert to the Catholic Church in the fifties. Events from the last half century have consolidated the tickles into the realization that I must learn everything I can. The theologies of religions and value clarification are in McClownee's realm; mathematics and physics are in Mickey's realm. This book comes from the four main tickles that most challenged me to be enlightened: Not one of these areas of knowledge was alone responsible for the feather tickling, as in, "Ah, now I know all about physics."

This book addresses the problems of abuse, whether physical, emotional, sexual, intellectual, or any other form. Abuse became prominent in my thinking when I retired. The problems of abuse in my life were there when I first started teaching, and they were prevalent from the time I was born. However, I had little time to examine those problems. I had many other issues rearing their heads in my day-to-day life: I was learning to be a husband; I was learning to be a dad; I was learning to teach the thirty or so students in my classroom; I was learning how to learn. I did not take the time or have the inclination at that time to deal with my deeper problems or other people's problems of abuse.

I grew up in a dysfunctional family. My alcoholic father neglected or rejected me. I saw him occasionally when he was sober, rarely when drunk. My mother worked afternoons and evenings to make ends meet. As a result, I did not see much of her. I was pretty much on my own, so I skipped from one role model to another. I was afraid of being neglected or rejected.

Consequently, in some weird, perverse, illogical way of thinking, I neglected and rejected others. All of us in some way rationalize to justify our behavior. We blame others for our behavior. Somehow, I managed to stop blaming others or myself for my behavior

During the1970s, the tickling feather started to form an altruistic desire to help people of all ages as they encounter and (hopefully) overcome abuse in any of its many forms. I have counseled many students on how to cope with their specific needs.

My wife of fifty-five years, Janet Lee Blair, agreed to marry me in 1953. This was my introduction to values. She has strong values that guide her, and they stay constant. She believes in tradition. She believes in riddles. She talks in metaphors. She is dyslexic and worked hard to learn to read. She has always believed in me. She supported my dreams all through our college and university days, and she raised our five kids, as well as me, with my personas of McClownee and Mickey that make up my personality. She is my partner in writing this book.

The calamity by priests in the Catholic Church, especially in San Diego and Tucson, brought the problem of abuse back to me full force when I retired in 1996. The tickle became a torrent of feathers, and this book began to take form.

The real epiphany occurred one evening when I was talking on the phone to my son Greg. I found myself staring at the picture on my office wall of Jesus talking to a little boy. The title of the picture is "Teach Me to Walk in Your Light." I realized that all of the knowledge in my head was His light. I started writing this book about Jesus teaching a little boy how to overcome his abuse by learning about his gifts as a person. The boy learns of the light.

This book is my portrayal of Jesus as a teacher, friend, and spiritual father of the little boy. The story covers about twelve years of the boy's life, as he grows into his late teens. The boy gains knowledge of the words, ideas, thoughts, and language of the heroes and idols that have tickled my mind and feelings over the years. As a teacher, I taught about the giants of the present time, and those that came before us. We learn from their original works. This book is the accumulation of their ideas. I can only say that I trust and believe in the truth of their words and language.

I truly believe that it is through learning that we as human beings will overcome the many forms of abuse and torture. We achieve a state of self-esteem and self-respect by expanding our hearts and minds. I am asking the readers of this book to seek this state. Learn by reading to yourself and others.

May this book provide hope, guidance, and consolation to all those who are in need. You are not alone!

Papa's Note to the Family

My main value is Enlightenment. I have spent a lifetime seeking its fulfillment. I have tried to define it as being broad-minded and wise, with an imaginative intellect. I have tried to act within it by being forgiving, responsible, honest, and lawful. I set my goals and dreams to achieve it.

The feather tickling increased my ambitious desire to be more enlightened. McClownee and Mickey, my fashioned friends, were like angels sitting on my shoulders and acting as my conscience, leading me to be enlightened. They also represent the left and right hemispheres of my brain.

I felt abused when I was neglected or rejected. I took it upon myself to be enlightened about abuse. I learned quickly the general concept that all forms of abuse come from those people who seek power. Long ago, I wrote an ode to power as my emotional promise to students:

I have no power over you.
Nor do you have any power over me.
True power is that which we share with each other by consent.
Misuse of power is trying to control or manipulate others to do our
greedy, selfish, self-centered will.

The Power of Power

The Man and a Boy was written to illustrate the dark side of power, as in the following statements:

Misuse of power in:
    brutalizing of young children
    molestations of boys and girls
    rape of women
    spousal abuse
    emotional manipulation
    threats to intellectual abilities
    the areas of race, religion, or gender

The Man and a Boy was written to illustrate the bright side of power, as in the following statements:

Proper use of power in:
    forgiving the self and others
    forgiving abusers, but not the act
    compassionate mercy to pardon
    describing languages
    the rule of laws
    the creation of the universe
    describing the areas of love
    healing bodies, transforming hearts, and fulfilling its mandate
to forgive

The Man and a Boy was written with the hope that our families would be aware of and forever understand the concept of power.

Introduction

The boy is of the greatest importance in this story. Whoever becomes like a child is of the greatest importance in the reign. By paraphrasing the Bible, The Man assures us that unless we change and become like little children, we will not enter the kingdom.

"Anyone who welcomes one little child like this in my name welcomes me," says The Man, speaking from Matthew 18, verses 5-6[1] "But anyone who is the downfall of one of these little ones who have faith in me would be better drown in the depths of the sea with a great millstone around his neck!" The Man changed the next words to help the boy understand. "Nothing but terrible things will come on a person through the scandal of torture and abuse!"

The abused little boy comes from a dysfunctional family, the father beating the boy without mercy. The immature eight-year-old boy was becoming a demon. He could not lash out at the world, so he would destroy himself, either by learning to hate with evil and ugly behaviors, or by constantly thinking about falling over the precipice into the abyss of suicide.

These debasing themes are paramount in Dialogues. The degradation by abuse and the horrid torture by crucifixion are the ultimate challenges the boy and The Man have faced, respectively. Abuse, crucifixion, and torture are the most ghastly experiences of butchery on any human being, and are experienced by thousands who are coerced to walk in the shoes of The Man and a boy. The problem of abuse is epidemic.

The Man comes into the boy's life, playing many roles to help the boy overcome his own destruction. He helps the boy to be a child of God. He wants the boy to think and feel that he is of great importance. The Man constantly encourages the boy to change and be like a little child. He assists the boy in doing this by attaining the Wisdom of Solomon and having faith.

Many wonderful moments of conversation occur between them. The boy learns to listen with his heart, mind, and soul. He learns the value of hard work. He learns to free himself of unwanted baggage and pay attention. The boy eventually realizes the value of enlightenment and the wisdom of unconditional love.

In their Dialogues, the boy is worthy of The Man's affection and time. He becomes the inquisitive student, forever asking the challenging questions. The boy learns to see The Man as the perfect model. He feels good about spending time together with The Man. He grows from an immature eight-year-old to a knowledgeable nineteen-year-old. The Man becomes his teacher, his friend, and ultimately his spiritual father.

They share ideas and values. The boy learns words from many languages. He learns to think and understand concepts from the simple to the complex. The boy learns to recognize and work toward solving his psychological problems.

Answering his many questions gives rise to other themes and topics during the Dialogues. Numerous topics come from the Bible. Various topics come from Nobel Prize winners and other notable scientists. The topics involving science are understandable when read with an open mind and a little perseverance. It is important that the boy learn the sciences.

McClownee and Mickey produce two major characters: The Man and the boy. The main traits of The Man are around ninety-five percent those of a human personality. That is why Jesus is called "The Man." The vast majority of these traits are achievable for all humans. The other five percent would fall into a supernatural spirituality. The Resurrection of The Man was the result of His Crucifixion.

The boy is a bright, cocky little imp who finally begins to strive for the deepest meanings of those human traits by observing and learning from the personality of The Man. He struggles trying to find his gifts. From reading the Bible, he learns to ask the same question as the disciples, and gets the same answer. "Who is of the greatest in the Kingdom of Heaven?" Matthew 18, verses 1,5[2]: "Anyone who welcomes one little child like this in my name welcomes me!" The enlightenment of the boy is the result of his abuse, as told in the Dialogues.

Prologue

The Man unexpectedly appears in a tree-shaded garden, where light flickers, filtering through the leaves. He is standing slightly behind the largest tree, barely visible in the shade. He is intently watching a wretched young boy sobbing away.

Bobbing on the soft mulchy ground in a rigid sitting fetal position, the boy is pain. His arms wrap around his bent-up knees, with his head in his hands between his knees. The tears are mixed with blood and drenching the mulch.

The Man cannot clearly see the boy's face; however, it appears to be beaten, battered, and swollen, with black and blue bruises.

Stiffly rocking back and forth, the boy is retching the blood, tears, and spit from his nose and mouth. A few deep cuts in his brows and a huge gash on his cheek under his left eye are severe enough to require stitches. The cuts contribute to the ugliness of the violence the boy has met head-on. His fight for life is almost gone.

The Man has seen enough. His heart goes out to the boy. He slowly approaches the boy. He does not want to terrify him. He quietly sits on the large boulder just behind the boy.

The Man's long, wavy brown hair hangs loose on his shoulders. It captures his face and enhances his handsome features. Upon his bearded face, a caring, compassionate look brings serenity to the moment.

He wants the boy to feel secure. He bends over and gently pats the boy's shoulder. The boy cowers at the touch. It appears to The Man that the boy expects a physical thumping. The boy falls to his side and bundles up tighter into his fetal position. He is completely submissive. The Man is more than a little concerned that the boy is contemplating suicide.

The Man starts to hum. His tone of voice is a soft, low baritone, barely loud enough to declare the words.

Through his gloominess, the boy feels the song as well as hears the words. He remembers someone singing to him a soothing lullaby a long time ago. Maybe it was his mother. For sure, it wasn't his drunken, brutal father. The words of the song he is hearing feel different from the song he feels in his heart. He hears words, in his thoughts, from Matthew 11:28–30[3]: *Come to me, all you who labor and are overburdened, and I will give you rest. Shoulder my yoke and learn from me, for I am gentle and humble of heart, and you will find rest for your soul. Yes, my yoke is easy and my burden light.*

In his heart, the boy feels a song with a weird language he's never heard before. He feels his heart is listening to a love song. His anguish is being soothed. He never felt anything like this before.

The Man repeats the song over and over again. Each coda is more soothing than the last. The boy tries to open his eyes to see who is humming. One of his eyes is swollen shut. The other eye sees a blurry figure wrapped in smoke. He has to unravel his body to get a better look.

The Man appears strong to the boy. Even though The Man is sitting, he appears tall. *He looks bigger than my old man,* thought the boy. *Maybe I could get Him to beat up my drunken dad.* He thought of the evilest revenge against his father.

The Man looks strange. New words describing an image seem to come into the boy's head. The words tell of The Man wearing clean clothing, like an old, faded dusty-red robe that covers His clean one-piece unbleached white muslin gown. Thin straps hold sandals to His dusty bare feet. He has no socks. His long fingers rest on His thighs. The Man and His clothes cast a simple, dazzling aura.

The boy, with difficulty, rises back into a sitting position. He stays in a tight pose. He still can only see a blurry image through the one eye. He turns his head and spits out a bloody mouthful of gunk. It takes a minute to clear his mouth and nose so he can talk. Even then, the words sound and smell like a gargling cesspool. Even in his submissive state, he comes up with enough oomph to act out.

Becoming his typical smart-ass self, he gushes out the words through swollen lips: "Oo da hell are you?" It hurts to talk. But he isn't going to give up without a fight. He pauses. "How come you're wearin' dos dirty ol' clothes?"

He gasps in a deep breath and chokes on his own spit. After coughing and spitting out still more bloody gunk, he forces out the barely incoherent words: "Dey look like dey came from some ol' trash bin. Wha' ya do, rip 'em off some ol bum on skid row?"

He is trying to put The Man down. However, The Man smiles at him with happy eyes. The boy is leery, his first impression is enough to let the boy know that The Man has a warm heart.

The boy straightens his legs and looks at his own clothes. They are bloody, torn, and caked with dirt. He wobbles and falls over as he tries to stand up. He tries again. With The Man's help, he succeeds. His eyes are below the level of the sitting Man's chin.

Here he is, this snotty boy, small for just eight years old, clad in filth, standing next to a handsome man with weird, neat, clean clothes. The boy feels shame. One thing his mother did do was nag him about being clean. The Man is clean. The boy feels totally worthless, dirty, and ugly, both on the inside and outside.

The man tilts and bows his head in admiration. The boy's head, with his half-closed eyes, rises up with a new reverence. Their connected eyes reflect the high regard each has for the other on this first meeting. The Man's slightly raised eyebrows allow the mysterious twinkle in his eyes to express the unconditional love he has for the boy.

With his left hand reaching out lovingly to the boy's shoulder, he cradles the boy gently in his left arm. His right hand soothingly pushes the boy's hair back off his eyes. The Man's right thumb gently wipes the tears and blood from the boy's eyes. His touch indicates to the boy His full-undivided attention and unconditional love. The boy doesn't know the words to convey this, *but he feels good.*

The boy frees his arms and elbows from The Man's hug. His hands reach up and open in a supplicating manner. The boy wants to touch The Man's face. There is brilliance about The Man, which comes from his innermost being. The Man's brightness reflects his glory. The boy's countenance emanates confusion and bafflement.

In all his crudeness, the boy wants to understand why he feels that this Man loves him. He reverts to a time when he was an innocent little boy. He had seen a picture of Jesus. With this image in his mind, *The Man's arms were the Holy Spirit rocking him like a loved baby.* The Holy Spirit appears to be listening to the coos and aahs of the little boy. The boy had forgotten this picture. But he now remembers his mom pointing at the title and reading it to him. He says the words aloud. "Thus the story begins. Teach me to walk in your light[4]."

CHAPTER ONE
A small, immature eight-year-old kid

Dialogue One
The Brutality of the Dad

The Man spoke for the first time. "Let us walk over to the little pond and get you cleaned up." As they walked, The Man put his hand gently on the boy's shoulder. "Do you want to talk about what happened to you?" he asked.

"Sure, why the hell not! My dad beat the shit out of me!" It surprised the boy that his words came out normally. He reached up and felt his face. It felt okay. The Man kept quiet, patiently waiting.

After a while, the boy said in an angry tone, "My dad was drunk, as usual. He came home with no money, no food, nothing. Oh, he had his pint bottle of muscatel wine in his back pocket. My mom started yelling at him. She called him all kinds of names. He told her to shut the hell up. She tried to slap him, but he liked to fight when he was drunk. He blocked her slap, and then slapped her back. He kept slapping her with one hand as he held her up with the other.

"I tried to stop him. I jumped on his back and tried to grab his arm so he couldn't hit her anymore. He let go of her and threw me off him. I bounced on the floor. Then he got down on his knees and came after me. He said what he always said when he was supposedly going to teach me to box. 'Come on, big shot, let's box! I'm your size. Put your dukes up, boy!'"

The Man and the boy reached the pond. Very carefully, with great empathy and sensitivity, The Man helped the boy out of his dirty clothes. The boy was a little self-conscious about being naked in front of The Man. One of the things his dad taught him when they were in the skid row slums was to "*be leery of perverts!*"

The boy saw that he had bruises all over his body. He tested the water with his toe. *He was surprised by how warm it was. It felt so good!* "I usually don't take baths, except on Saturday nights. I remember the Saturday night when a big rat jumped out from under the bathtub and scared the living be Jesus out of my mother." The Man slowly shook his head and gave a wry grin.

As the boy got out of the warm pond, he noticed all his bruises were gone. Both eyes opened. He could see. He picked up his clothes, and they were all clean and as good as new. He couldn't believe his eyes. He got a little scared, wondering what the Man was doing. They started to return to the garden, and The Man asked the boy to finish telling Him how he got the bruises.

The boy again became leery of what The Man wanted, but when The Man smiled at him, the boy's fears were overcome. He was okay. "Anytime my dad wanted to teach me a lesson, he would whip me with his belt until I had welts. Or he would beat me senseless while teaching me to box. Well, last night was a boxing lesson. You saw my body. I'm surprised the bruises went away so quick. It usually takes a week or so. Then my dad teaches me more lessons, and I get more bruises. Sometimes I got a few broken ribs, a broken arm or leg, and I had to go the hospital. That's the end of the story!"

The boy fell silent, obviously withdrawing in thought for a time. Suddenly, tears started to trickle down his cheeks. "Except this time I thought I'd run away and stay in the garden. I didn't think anyone would find me here. Say, how come you found me? You're not a pervert, are you? You're not going to hurt me?"

Dialogue Two
Hanging Out

"No! I will never hurt you," The Man quietly promised. "I will stay in the garden with you for a while. I would like to show you what it is like to have a real, loving dad. We can learn many things together. We can hang out."

"Are you going to be my dad?" the boy asked sarcastically, trying to hide his fright.

The Man answered serenely, "Yes … I am your Heavenly Father!"

The boy's countenance again showed confusion and bafflement. The Man was puzzling. *So what,* the boy thought. *I like puzzles and riddles.* Always afraid of being beaten or abused, the boy asked, "Where's my real dad? Are you going to leave me and go get drunk like he did?" The boy's questions constantly had a scornful scorpion-like stinger attached to them. He used questions to intimidate others by playing little put–down games.

"I will never leave you, nor will I ever reject you! I will always be with you in the Kingdom of God," said The Man. His compelling manner was so charismatically comforting that the boy started to cry.

He tried to wipe away tears without The Man noticing. He didn't want The Man to think he was a big sissy. Deep inside his heart, he felt questions: *Who is this Man? Do I know Jesus?* He said in a mocking whisper, "I don't know what the Kingdom of God means." Deep inside his mind, he again heard these questions: *Who is this Man? Do I know Jesus?*

The Man answered in a kind, gentle, loving manner. "You will learn about the Father, Me, and the Holy Spirit."

The boy retorted harshly, "Oh yeah? I don't like people telling me what I got to do or what I got to learn!"

"That's okay," The Man stated. "A foolish faith in authority is the worst enemy of truth."

With reckless pride, the boy replied angrily, "I don't know if I understand your words! I don't need you or anybody! I can do it all by myself."

The Man again spoke gently. "I will always be there with My love. I will teach you to walk in My light. I will teach you to *be*!"

The boy snickered. "That's just great! But how will I know you are there? Will you talk to me … like now?" The boy was actually pleading with The Man to like him, but his tone was raucous and resentful.

The Man answered softly, touching the boy's heart. "I will show you many ways that 'love is a better teacher than a sense of duty'. Together we will fine a way to measure love."

The boy felt sorry for himself. "Nobody really loves me. You can say all you want about love, but I don't know if I believe it. People will think I'm crazy talking to you." Deep inside, his soul yearned. For the third time, his heart, mind, and soul asked those same questions: *Who is this Man? Do I know Jesus?*

The Man felt remorse for the boy. He said, "You will be tempted as I was. The devil tempted Me three times! Peter denied Me three times."

"Where's da love?" the boy asked sardonically. "How will I know that I'm tempted and love will save me? How will I measure love?"

Dialogue Three
Past Memories and Future Goals

The boy just had to be a smart aleck. He repeated the questions. "Where's da love? How will I know that I'm tempted and love will save me?"

The Man sat silently. He looked at the boy with that twinkle in his eyes, and in the most loving, caring manner, he softened the hurtful, harsh feelings of the boy with these words: "I know that a new laptop computer is not a love object, nor is it a substitute for affection. However, I want us to look at some video pictures from a CD in the folder titled 'An Abused boy's Life.' The video is graphic and violent. This could be you if you choose to give in to your abuse."

He handed the computer to the boy. "Do you need me to boot it up?"

The boy sneered at The Man. "I can boot it up. I'm not dumb!" Many video pictures were framed within a given theme of abuse, and no sound emanated as the computer scrolled through the video.

The first frame showed a young boy around ten years old breaking into a school and trashing a classroom. The police caught him, and he appeared before a juvenile judge. They detained him in juvenile hall. He spent most of his time in a silent cell. After his release from juvenile hall, the angry, out-of-control dad whipped his boy with a wooden strop coated with leather. With the young boy curled up in the corner of a room, the video pictures faded away.

The second frame of video pictures was about the same young boy. He was now about eleven years old. He built a secret fort in the rafters of a lumberyard building. The police caught and convicted him of trespassing and arson. The arson charge was for candles the boy used in the fort, which could have started a fire in the lumberyard. The father again whipped the boy with the strop.

A third frame of video images depicted the same boy a little older, breaking into parking meters for nickels and dimes.

The fourth frame showed the same boy stealing a bike. At the end of each of the frames of video, the father whips the boy with the strop.

The Man reached over to pause the video. He looked at the boy, who was very perplexed. After a long period of silence, He restarted the video.

The fifth frame showed the boy, now fourteen or fifteen, stealing beer, wine, and whiskey from stores.

The same boy, at sixteen years old, received his driver's license. The police stopped him for reckless, drunken driving and disorderly conduct in a stolen car. The judge took his driver's license away and put him in juvenile hall again. When he finally got home, the father whipped him with the strop until the blows brought bloody welts graphically shown in the video.

The Man then asked the boy, "Do you see from the videos that the boy's life is full of anger and rage? Do you see the boy becoming evil and learning to hate?" The Man hesitated. "Would you like to see more?"

The boy remained quiet. The pictures started again, with a set about snatching an old lady's purse; a set about drugs that covered a two-year span; a set involving fistfights, where the boy brutalized younger and smaller boys and girls; a set about a narcissistic, lying, cheating scamp.

The last frame of pictures started with the boy standing on the corner of a street in the slums. A few streetlights were on. The night was cold. He stood with his hands deep in his pockets. A few female prostitutes walked up and down the street. Standing next to a rundown set of stairs that led to the front door of a boarded-up row house was a disheveled boy prostitute.

A late-model limousine pulled up to the curb. The darkly tinted right rear window whirred down. The boy stepped to the open window and leaned in the open space. All heads turned toward the car as the crack of the bat resonated as soundless thunder in the silent video. The boy fell, the back of his head crashing against the concrete. The streetlight reflected his bruised, battered, bloodied, scarred face. His nose was out of place. A flashily dressed man stepped out of the car and kicked the boy in the ribs.

The Man stopped the gruesome video. He knew the young eight-year-old boy had seen enough.

The information inundated the boy's thoughts. The frames of the video pictures were bouncing around in his head. His body felt as if it had a ten-ton weight on it. Then The Man's voice broke through the miasmic mist of pollution that was surrounding the boy's heart, mind, and soul.

The Man said, "You do not have to become this boy in the videos. Know that I will empower you, helping you to overcome any thoughts of destroying yourself. I will give you the strength to forget the evil, ugly, tortured, violent abuse you have experienced.

"When you are about nineteen years old, I will send you your soul mate. She will help you develop your major values in life. She will give you the security you need to learn all about riddles and mysteries and the understanding to solve them. You will learn to value enlightenment above all things. You will gain understanding and wisdom; however, it will take you many years to overcome the influence and sting of your abused pride. You can grow to be a man in the fullest sense.

"You are truly, innately clever, but it will take faith and hard work with good actions to overcome your many temptations. You will finally come to realize that you are smart, but without guidance from the Father, you will still do those things that will keep you in the clutches of potential disaster.

"You may not understand at this moment all that I said. However, let us start your lessons. In your laptop computer, I will type everything from the simplest ideas to the more complex major values and themes you will be required to learn so you can walk in My light. You will also be required to learn the rules to many different subjects. For example, English and Spanish, algebra and geometry, as well as biology and physics, are ways of communicating and ways of thinking. As your teacher, I expect full obedience."

Inside himself, the boy still posed the questions: *Who is this Man? Do I know Jesus?* Yet, he retorted with resentment, "What do you think I am, a dog who just obeys because you train him? You give me a brand-new laptop computer and you think I'm just going to kowtow to your every whim?" The boy then realized he was repeating his mom's words when she got mad at his dad. Although she used these words: "You think I'm supposed to spread my legs at your every whim."

The Man tried to break through the false veneer. "You have the gift of inner sensitivity that enables you to see and hear the subtle signs that our Father sends to break the dictatorship of convention. You will build new traditions with your soul mate. You will learn to obey the truth. You will learn to mourn."

The boy interrupted, "What's that mean? I'll like going to funerals and kissing the dead like Huck did? Yeah! I know about Huck and Tom using funny words. I liked the stories."

Dialogue Four
Emotions, Feelings, Future, and Truth

"What's mourning?" asked the boy. "I remember the story about Huck Finn where he saw a corpse in a casket. They told him it was proper to mourn and kiss the dead at funerals. That freaked me out."

"No!" The Man countered. "Kissing the dead is not mourning. Kissing the dead is a custom in some cultures to overcome the fear of death. Fear brings a painful feeling of misery and agony. Painful feelings are associated with the impending danger or evil of the devil. If you kiss a corpse, you are supposed to kiss away fear."

The Man directed the boy's thoughts to the beatitudes. "Mourning is something else. It means that you will feel true sorrow and grief for all living things when they die. I died on the cross for your redemption. Death and dying will bring deep emotional tears to your eyes.

"You will mourn the death of old ways, old traditions, and outdated laws. You will not hold on to them. You will feel sorrow and grief as you let them pass. Learning new rules and new laws brings you joy. You need not fear the past. The past is gone. You will understand the flow of time. You look for the new in the future. The Resurrection and overcoming abuse are joyful; the present and the future bring new light."

The Man's voice changed from a tone of reassurance to one of possible foreboding. "The evil and dark aspects of mourning means you lose all hope; you become mistrustful of love and truth. This kind of hateful mourning will eat away at you and destroy you from within. It is the evil that comes with abuse."

The Man paused. You could hear the wind rustle the leaves of the trees. He broke the silence in a slightly lighter tone of voice. "If you obey My teaching, you will have a shattering encounter with truth, which will lead to true conversion and the power to resist evil. I will teach you to mourn with hope and love and to see the truth."

Defiantly, the boy shot back, "I'm only an eight-year-old kid! How am I supposed to know all these words that you're saying?" He used his fists to bang his head repetitively. The Man gently grabbed his wrists and pulled the boy to his chest.

The boy shrieked at The Man. He wanted to blame The Man for all the bad things that happened to him. "You showed me those scary videos. They were creepier then seeing Huck kiss the dead. If you're my Heavenly Father, why are You letting the devil do all these bad things to me? I meet him every time my dad hits me. He calls me a devil. He says he needs to beat the evil shit out of me. Why don't you just stop my dad? Why don't you zap me and make me good!"

The Man's demeanor was comforting, and he spoke softly. "You are not poor in spirit! You have the freedom to choose and satisfy your own will. You think you are a child in poverty because you feel that no one loves you. Nevertheless, you have the moral attitude required for heaven if you learn to treat others, as you would like them to treat you. I want you to direct your hunger and thirst for righteousness through Me. Search for something great, like true justice, true good, or true reality."

Continuing in his gentle ways, The Man said, "The Father's will is for you to seek the natural laws and understand the inspiration of the prophets. The Kingdom of God in Matthew[5] is the reassertion of the laws. Read and reread the beatitudes to understand your gifts. Work hard, do your best, and fill yourself with knowledge. When you enter the Kingdom of Heaven, the Father will be pleased. You will be applauded."

The Man left the boy in the garden, with the promise that he would return whenever the boy ran into trouble. The boy learned to talk and listen to The Man through his prayers. He followed the directions on his computer. He did well. He went back to school and worked hard on his studies. He stayed shy of his dad, and for some reason, his dad did not physically abuse him. But he did still yell at him, telling him how stupid he was because he was just learning to read, and that he would never amount to anything.

However, his short visits with The Man in the garden over the next seven years pulled him through the bad times he experienced until he was fifteen.

CHAPTER TWO
A fifteen–then sixteen-year-old boy is a narcissistic teenager

Dialogue Five
Moral and Natural Laws = Faith

The Man's first words to the boy on his fifteenth birthday were, "You are not poor in spirit. You have the freedom to choose and satisfy your own will." The Man repeated this statement with authority. His manner was pure confidence and wisdom. He quoted Matthew 5:17–18[6] to bring the boy back to the here and now about the laws.

"Do not imagine that I have come to abolish the Law or the Prophets. I have come not to abolish but to complete them. In truth I tell you, till heaven and earth disappear, not one dot, not one stroke, is to disappear from the Law until all its purpose is achieved."

The Man said to the boy, "Given to you, with hope and love, is our will of the law. Receiving it is your will." He continued in His unbelievable manner. "I want you to fulfill and spend your life teaching the commands of the scientific laws. I want you also to study the Bible and gain knowledge of the moral laws. The principles of faith in the moral laws are in fact complimentary with the principles of science. There is a richly satisfying harmony between the scientific and spiritual worldviews.

"God's domain is the spiritual world: a realm defined by the heart, the soul, and the mind. Science's domain is nature. However, God does not exclude Himself from natural laws. Faith and science exist together in the Kingdom of God."

The boy became confused and frustrated. "I don't know. I don't think I can do what you say!" He tried, but he couldn't impersonate the confidence of The Man. He was floundering like a fish out of water. His inclination for secrecy and the narcissistic mind-set of a fifteen year old almost stopped him from confessing his feelings. He remembered the videos. He reverted to his defensive imagination and created all sorts of exaggerated sharp retorts. "You're telling me that I will become a quitter 'cause my dad abused me. You're saying I will get in fights, smoke, drink booze, and do drugs 'cause I was abused. You're saying that because he would leave me to go get drunk, in turn, I will screw people around before they can screw me.

"If I hear you right, I'm afraid to try something 'cause I think I'm going to make a jackass of myself and fail. You say I act stupid, talking trash and blaming others for my failures. My so-called friends make fun of me because I'm mean. I'm self-conscious, so I show off to gain attention. I get in fights just to show I can box and beat up guys. I can even come up with a lot of dumb words."

All of a sudden, the boy's thoughts clouded up. An image of The Man flared in his mind. Again the questions—*Who is this Man? Do I know Jesus?*—echoed deep inside his being.

The Man looked down at him with loving sorrow. Here was a narcissistic, suffering young man, one of God's children, berating himself with phony pride. The Man was full of empathy for the pathetic young man.

"Oh what little faith. It will take a little while. With all your self-pity, you make the road harder to travel. Using hurtful words, accusing others of misdeeds, judging others, and throwing temper tantrums reflects your false pride."

Again, after a few silent moments, The Man spoke: "I want you to be my friend. I will be there with love and encouragement. You will recognize the moments when we are communicating, so don't be afraid."

He hesitated, giving the boy time to reflect. "Eventually your peers will label you the consummate teacher. I wrote in your laptop computer the major themes I want you to learn so you can walk in My light. "Now it is time for you to go back to your home and family and learn to be a man."

They sat in silence for a long time. The Man rose and walked out of the garden, leaving the boy in the subdued sunlight that flickered through the trees.

It had been a year since they'd last met in the garden. The boy's voice had changed. He was taller. He had pimples on his face. He was almost through puberty. He was getting some muscles. He was trying to stay out of trouble as he was growing up. His father no longer abused him physically or emotionally.

The Man had kept his promise. During the past years, the boy had recognized the moments when they talked. As part of their last conversation, they'd planned this meeting in the garden. At the silent bidding of The Man, the boy returned to the garden.

He looked over at The Man sitting on the rock. He hadn't changed a bit. The Man smiled at him and said, "Get your Bible out so we can continue to understand the beatitudes, the law, and the prophets. Through knowledge, you shall become a child worthy of the kingdom."[7]

Dialogue Six
Reading, Language, and the Medium

The sixteen-year-old boy repeated the words as he wobbled his head from side to side, imitating sneering, sarcastic responses, he had often heard his peers make. For some unknown reason, the boy reverted to acting like a smart aleck to The Man. "Go to your Bible! Study and understand the beatitudes! Learn about the law and the prophets! Be a child of God."

He was hesitant. He felt a great need again to confess to The Man his lack of speed and lousy vocabulary when reading. He blurted out, "I don't read very good! I stopped reading when I was twelve, in the seventh grade." He hung his head in humiliation. He became bashful. "The teachers made fun of me. They called me a dunce for asking stupid questions.

"When I did work hard and struggled reading the book *Two Years Before the Mast,* Mrs. Andrews said I cheated, that I didn't read the book. She accused me of having someone else write the book report. I hated that lady! I called her a bitch and ran from the classroom.

"My mom had to go to school and talk to the principal before I could go back to school. My mom always used guilt to make me behave. She would say, 'Damn it, why do you do this to me.' But you know something? I do love her. She tries."

The Man gave his usual friendly smile. "Don't fret the words in the Bible. Read what you can and ask questions. I'll be there in your heart to answer. Listen with your heart!" The Man picked up the Bible and started reading John 1:1–3[8] but read it to imitate the boy's style. "In the beginning was the Word. I am the Word. I am the Logos that gives light. I was with the Father before the beginning. I can handle stupid questions. The greatest dunce, the devil—with his tricks, tests, trials, and temptations—is no big problem. You can handle him with my help." The Man paused for a few minutes, watching the boy's reactions. The boy was agitated. He was such a hot head, and he was ready to act out.

"Here is what we are going to do! We are going to use your imagination. Seeing pictures in your mind is your best trait. Imagine that we first created a medium that will serve as the place where all the languages are stored. It is like the hard drive in your computer. Just picture the Father, Son, and Holy Spirit having fun creating the initial conditions of the universe with just the right constants.[9] All our plans were stored in the medium, along with the languages of mathematics.

"Imagine the joy we had in creating. Think of how we fine-tuned every aspect of the universe. Our creation had, and has, the ability to evolve into something that is so awe-inspiringly beautiful."

Dialogue Seven
Rage, Words, and Math

The Man began their lesson by handing the Bible to the boy. He asked the boy to read the words.

The boy was obviously anxious. He imagined the joy The Man had in creating the medium like a hard drive. He was down right jealous. He resented the fact that he couldn't read. He started reading haltingly: "What … has … come … into … being … in … him … was life, life that was the light of men—John 1:4–5[10]."

The Man added his own words with a little pride: "Sprinkled … with … truth … and … love."

Thinking The Man was making fun of him, the boy couldn't hold back his temper tantrum. He started ranting and raving. He threw the Bible to the floor. He screamed at The Man with the first words that came to his mind. "Boy, I didn't know anybody could be so full of words. You not only use big egghead words, but what are you, some wizard or magician? Are you one of those kinds of guys—soothsayers?—who predict stuff? You talk like mathematics is the only way to talk. How will I ever learn to talk like that? I don't even know if I want to learn that stuff.

"I already learned to add, subtract, and multiply by the third grade. What am I going to do, walk around all day saying one thing and two things equals three things. I asked my teacher why two plus two equals four, and she just said that's the way it is, so just do it and get the right answer. But how will I know that I'm getting the right answers? I asked her again. She said, 'You just know because things add up the right way.'

"Duh! boy, even I know that's a stupid answer! Okay, so I learned my multiplication tables and division and other math by the sixth grade—no big deal. I memorized the steps for long division—again, no big deal. When I got to division of fractions, I was told to invert and multiply to get the right answers. Again, I asked her why. I'll never forget Mrs. Andrews's answer: 'Just do it, because I'm the teacher and I'm telling you so.'"

The boy looked angrily at The Man. "So, you, Mr. Big Words,

The Man and a Boy

you want to teach me. You say all I have to do is obey you and walk in your light, whatever that means! If I walk with you, I will learn the truth. Big frigging deal!" The agitation and anger kept building, and he shouted louder. "Man, you know what my boozing daddy would say to that bullshit? You can't get to first base with that shit!"

His seething started cooling off a little. "Although I will admit that when my Dad was sober, he could shoot a good game of pool: eight ball, snooker, or nine ball. He taught me the angles for three-cushion billiards. I guess that's math."

His perturbation was waning. His voice softened. "You know, maybe I am being dumb!" A revelation descended upon him. "If my alkie father could teach me to play pool, play baseball, and box, maybe you could be my teacher. You're nicer and have a better smile. My dad was mean, and he beat me a lot. He pays no attentions to me now. He just calls me a dumb shit. Promise you won't be mean to me like my dad."

Dialogue Eight
Tower of Babel and Language

The Man waited patiently for the boy to continue his thoughts. The boy said, "Okay, I'll try to learn all that stuff you put in the computer, but I can't learn stuff just because you say so. I want to know why. Like, why is two and two four? I think I can do the math, but I have trouble with words." The Man opened His Bible to Genesis 11:1–9[11], "The Tower of Babel." He handed the open Bible to the boy.

"Read," He softly commanded. The boy looked at The Man, pleading with his eyes. The boy was so self-conscious about his inability to read. The Man smiled at the boy as only He could smile. The boy started reading haltingly. Nonetheless, he gained confidence with each word. "The … whole … world … spoke … the … same language, with the same … vocabulary."[11]

The boy skipped a line and then started again with confidence. "They said to one another, 'Come let us make bricks and bake them in fire.' For stone they used bricks, and for mortar they used bitumen."[11] The boy looked up at The Man. "What's bitumen?"

"It is a tar-like substance, an asphalt that glues the bricks together," The Man said.

The boy found his place and continued reading a little more smoothly. 'Come,' they said, 'let us build ourselves a city and a tower with its top reaching heaven.[11] 'Let us make a name for ourselves, so that we do not get scattered all over the world.'[11] The boy looked at The Man for reassurance. The Man smiled. The boy read on from the Bible. "Now Yahweh came down to see the city and the tower that the people had built.[11] 'So they are all a single people with a single language!' said Yahweh. 'This is only the start of their undertakings! Now nothing they plan to do will be beyond them. Come, let us go down and confuse their language there, so that they cannot understand one another.'"[11]

The boy looked at The Man and understood in his heart why he had to learn languages. He didn't want to be like his father; he wanted to be like The Man. He continued reading with more confidence than ever. The inflection in his voice was improving. He started to feel the language.

"Yahweh scattered them thence all over the world, and they stopped building the city. That is why it was called Babel, since Yahweh confused the language of the whole world; and from there Yahweh scattered them all over the world."[11] The boy asked The Man, "Am I reading okay?"

The Man again smiled and answered, "Yes, you read very well. You are improving each time you read. Do you understand why I ask you to read about the Tower of Babel?"

"Kind of," the boy answered. The Man kept quiet. After a while, the boy broke the silence and continued. "At Babel, the Lord confused the way people talked and scattered their languages all around the entire world. Otherwise they would have only the one language."

The boy started to read, but stopped. He appeared puzzled. "What was wrong with the way people talked?" He asked it as if it was a riddle to solve.

"The people had sinned," The Man replied.

"But what did they really do wrong, according to God?"

The Man answered in His most assertive manner. "Their sin was overweening pride, an act of insensate pride.[11] If they are one people, all speaking the same language, nothing will later stop them from doing whatever they presume to do, regardless of the consequences of their actions. They will exist in a box."

Dialogue Nine
Many Systems of Laws

The Man repeated the metaphor because the boy looked a little confused with the idea of people in a box. "When you think of people in a box, think of how they are limiting themselves. One language will build artificial walls around them, reducing their opportunities for growth. One language will lead them down a blind, evolutional alley. They will not be able to think outside the box. They limit themselves to narrow perspectives. It is like the game of tennis, played on a small court with rigid boundaries, a strict set of rules, and judges to enforce the rules."

With edginess, the boy responded, "Yeah! But wouldn't they be better off together, like a team?"

The Man marveled at the boy. "It will be up to me, as coach of the team, to unify the people. We want the people to develop their gifts so they will be worthy of being on the team. Multi-gifted people are less judgmental."

"But why confuse their language so that one person could not understand what another says?"

The Man responded authoritatively. "This was to teach the supremacy of God over human enterprises. The material means alone of building a single tower does not maintain unity amid men. We want to show that a single language isn't the best way for growth, for a people to evolve. A single language represents a single bias. It is a strong inclination, which prevents unprejudiced consideration of a question."

"So that's why you told me that a foolish faith in authority is the worst enemy of truth! 'Yes!'

"The Man laughed loudly, excited at the boy's understanding.

The boy continued, "So a single language and a single leader wouldn't get to know the truth."

The boy yelled eagerly, and his sixteen-year-old voice cracked. "So, to be like God, we humans must learn all the languages. This means all spoken ones, all the written ones, all the math and science ones, all the sign languages, and every one that God knows but has not yet invented by us."

"Oh, you are getting so smart." The Man laughed joyously.

The boy quietly, with a barely audible sound, reflected: "It will be hard for one person or even thousands to learn all the languages." He then raised his voice. "Let me see if I get this straight. Each person will learn as many languages as they can, and this will be their gift as a person. My gift is my imagination, where I see pictures rather than words. My picture words are also in the medium."

The Man was extremely satisfied with the boy's progress. "Yes! We created the medium for that purpose. The truth is in the medium. It is full of languages." The Man was analyzing the boy's body language as He continued speaking. "People will have to learn many languages to understand all the laws we formulated in creating the universe. The natural laws, the moral laws, the judicial laws, the constitutional Laws, the cultural mores, the mathematical laws, the scientific laws, and so on. All these laws and words are in the medium."

The Man went over the main points. "In the book of Genesis and in the Pentateuch, we had the prophet Moses write down what he could understand about the creation of the world and the moral laws. Now that humans are able to understand more of the creation, and its moral and social laws, we will help them, as children of God, to increase their knowledge through new technologies and math. As the computing power increases and speeds up, and the capacity for storing data increases, so will the ability to find solutions to more complex and difficult mathematical problems. The computer will be able translate solutions from one language to another."

CHAPTER THREE
A seventeen-year-old boy learns about time

Dialogue Ten
The Beginning of the boy's Education

The Man spoke directly to the boy, who was rapidly beginning to think more like a man—like The Man. "I want you to work hard to learn as much science and mathematics as you can. As your computing power increases, so will your ability to find solutions to the more difficult mathematical problems. You will be able to communicate in many different languages.

"I also want you to study the beatitudes: being gentle, mourning, hunger, and thirst for righteousness, and the pure in heart. This will balance you in the natural and moral systems. The more you learn, the better you will deal with abuse." The Man opened His Bible to John 1:9–12[12] He handed the open Bible to the boy. "Read," He said. The boy was becoming much more comfortable reading aloud, so he took the Bible in his hand.

"Getting to where you like to read, aren't you?" The Man laughed.

The boy gave an impish grin and read with confidence. "The Word was the real light that gives light to everyone; he was coming into the world. He was in the world that had come into being through him, and the world did not recognize him. He came to his own, and his own people did not accept him. But to those who did accept him, he gave power to become children of God."[12]

The boy looked up at The Man with a feeling that he had never felt before. He made eye contact and said quietly, "So you say God's domain is in the spiritual world. A realm examined with the heart, soul, and mind. So, when I ask a question, you will answer it in this spirit world?"

"No," said The Man. "You cannot exist in a spirit world beyond the earth. From now on, I will speak to your heart, soul, and mind. Just listen carefully as a child of God. You will be given wisdom beyond your seventeen years and be able to understand as you live on the earth.

He continued, directing the boy into one of the most intriguing areas of science: *time.* "Okay, let's try something simple. I have a motto; we will operate with 'KISS' as our guide. That stands for 'Keep it simple, student.' Do you know how to tell time?"

"Sure, with a clock," the boy replied.

"Pretty smart, aren't you? Any other ways?" The Man asked.

"I don't know!" the boy responded.

"How about your pulse?" The Man asked.

"Yeah! That might work, but sometimes it beats fast … and sometimes slow. I don't know if mine's the same as everybody's."

"Good answer," He praised. "Can you tell time by the sun?"

"Yeah, we say it takes a year for the earth to go around the sun."

"How about the moon?"

"Sure, the same idea. It takes a month for the moon to go around the earth!" answered the boy proudly.

"What's a day?"

His pride vanished. "I don't know. A day and a night?"

The Man asked, "What makes a day and a night?"

The boy finally got it. "Oh, now I know. It's when the sun rises, sets, and rises again."

The Man prodded him to explain his answer. "You seem to be mixed up. A minute ago, you said the earth goes around the sun, and now you are saying the sun moves by rising and setting. Do you mean the sun goes around the earth?"

"No. That's one of the things I figured out on my own. I'm a junior in high school, so I'm taking a class in physics. By Newton and Einstein's theories of gravity, the earth spins on its axis one time and makes it look like the sun is moving. The sun stays still."

"What exactly makes a year or a month?" The Man asked.

"A year is for the earth to go around the sun, and a month is for the moon to go around the earth."

"Can you feel the earth spinning on its axis or moving around the sun?"

"No, the earth is big!" replied the boy. "Too big for us to feel the motion. Like being in a big airplane. By Newton's law of inertia and Einstein's frame of reference, all motion is relative.

"Was it boring listening to and answering some questions about time?" asked The Man.

"Not really. I really like physics and astronomy."

Dialogue Eleven
The Arrow of Time[13]

"Let us walk," said The Man. He reached down, took the boy's hand in His, and pulled him up. They walked hand in hand from the shaded trees into the sunlight. The boy realized he was holding hands with The Man. It became real to him that he was a child of God. He was still a virgin. He liked girls, but they seemed to reject him, and most of them pissed him off. At least he knew he wasn't gay!

"Are you ready to listen again with your heart, soul, and mind, and not be bored?" The Man questioned him, hoping to receive only one answer.

"I will not be bored." The boy raised his and The Man's clasped hands into a high five and said with enthusiasm, "Okay, Let's find some more answers about time!"

"How many days in a month or in a year?" The Man asked.

As he looked at The Man with surprise, the boy answered, "Twenty-eight days and three hundred and sixty-five days."

"Are your answers accurate?"

"I don't know. I guess so. When I ask questions, people give me a hard time and make me feel like I'm stupid for asking questions. You act as if you want me to ask questions. In addition, you make me feel good. You make me feel smart. I even think I'm using the proper English."

"What if I told you there are different kinds of months? There's a solar, or calendar month, which is about one-twelfth of a year, or about thirty days. And a lunar, or a synodic, month, which is from one new moon to the next in twenty-nine days, twelve hours, forty-four minutes, and two point seven seconds."

"I didn't know!" said the boy. "What's the big deal?"

"Well, some people who call themselves creationists believe the earth is less than ten thousand years old, and they believe the first six days of creation were literally twenty-four-hour days."

"Whoa! So what's wrong with that?" Although the boy asked the question, he didn't care about an answer. He was just reverting to his long-practiced role of *I couldn't care less.* "How come we believe the scientists and not the creationist?" he finally asked.

The Man saw through the ruse and continued, "Scientists do experiments to validate their theories. They gather evidence and use accurate mathematical equations. Twenty-four-hour days are not accurate."

The boy was annoyed because he had no clue where these questions about time were going. "So why get so uptight and argue with the creationists over who's the most accurate?"

Deciding to stretch the boy's attention span a little, The Man said, "A year is three hundred and sixty-five days, but a leap year, every four years, has one day added. Then, every hundred years, they omit one day in the leap year. Scientists are constantly correcting their clocks to keep them accurate. They are also looking for newer clocks that are extremely accurate.

"Scientists depend on the integrity and repeatability of their theories and experiments," He continued. "Their mathematical language and solutions depend on the utmost accuracy. They use cesium atoms that vibrate under electrical applications. Scientist count the repetitive vibrations and have the most accurate clocks available."

He recognized he had reached the boy's limit of patience and understanding. He knew the boy was getting bored. He changed direction. "Let us say you are a clock. Take your pulse by putting your finger on your wrist. When you are sad or bored, you tick slowly. When you are happy or excited, you tick fast. Rarely during a day does your body tick regularly or consistently at the same pace."

"What are you saying? My body is a clock?" The thought of his body being a clock opened his mind to a vast number of questions and answers bouncing around in his head. He thought there must be a great number of riddles to solve. At seventeen, for instance, sex was a big riddle.

The Man recognized a teachable moment. He intuitively knew the boy's thoughts about sex. "Human beings are inaccurate clocks, and their similar experiences with other persons—about love and sex and their emotions—will seem different for each person. Now listen carefully," The Man directed. "The arrow of time is an illusion, and the world around each person is a figment of his or her imagination. From the beating of one's heart during waking or sleeping hours, to the dreams, daydreams, and fantasies during one's life, the arrow of time is different for each person.

"We, the Father, Son, and the Holy Spirit, created the first arrow of time over fourteen billion years ago. I am the Word! I am the Logos! I am Time!" He waited for the boy to think about what he'd just said. "Through the ages, there were mysterious questions about time: How short is time? How long is time? Does time have a beginning or an end? The concept of the arrow of time answers the first two questions about the short and long of time. The short is a second. The long is billions of years."[14]

Dialogue Twelve
I Am Time!

They had returned from their walk. The boy said, "Boy, here we go again with a lot of big words: *logos, mysterious, arrow of time,* and so on! How short is time? How long is time? Why are we spending so much time on time? Ha! That's a joke—time on time. Well," the boy continued, "does time have a beginning or end? Or does it just have a middle?" Again, he thought he was being funny.

The Man allowed the boy a few moments of self-serving humor. Then, with His hands on His hips in a strong authoritative stance, He looked down at the boy. He spoke persuasively. "The Father, Son, and Holy Spirit are the answer to that question. I will repeat the answer. "I am! I am the Word! I am the Logos! I have no beginning or end. I am Time!"

"Hold it right there!" the boy said arrogantly. "Do you mean to tell me that God is Time?"

The Man queried forcefully, "Do you believe that the earth goes around the sun?" He used the tact of misdirection.

For a few moments, the boy was puzzled. He thought he had to solve another riddle. "Well, yes! What's that got to do with God being Time?"

"Do you believe that all things exist in an arrow of time?" The Man asked. Again, he was misdirecting.

"I don't know. I guess! I don't know what an arrow of time means." The boy was obsessed with his fear of rejection. His compulsive behavior to sting like a scorpion dominated his seventeen-year-old mind-set.

The Man pardoned the boy patiently and responded gently. "Listen with your heart, soul, and mind. Use your imagination. Advance yourself mentally to an old age. Imagine a future son speaking to you from his heart to your heart. In an instant, which is now, you know about the arrow of time … and Time itself. You had an epiphany because I am the Word. I am Time everlasting. I am Time." He paused, then said, "Let's KISS!

"What's a minute?" The Man waited for the boy to answer.

"Ah, sixty seconds." The boy sensed The Man's kindness.

"What's a second?" The Man asked.

Hesitantly, he answered. "Uh, a tick of the second hand of a clock?"

"Okay! Is there anything smaller than a second?"

"I don't know, but now that you ask, I guess so."

"Do you believe that scientists can measure one one-hundredth of a millionth of a millionth of a millionth of a millionth of a millionth of a second?"

The boy's initial reaction was to reject The Man first, with sarcasm. He would show The Man he could be his own boss. He blurted out the next words that came to him with no feeling of regret. "Is this one of Mrs. Andrews's answers? Like, just do it, because I'm the teacher and I'm telling you so."

The Man smiled and said, "No, when you get older and are still studying physics, you will do experiments on the speed of light and the time it takes light to cross the diameter of a hydrogen nucleus. You will also do experiments that will prove that the earth spins on its axis in a day, and that the earth goes around the sun in a year."

The Man paused for a few moments, and then he started with a story, somewhat like a parable. "Imagine a sunny day, and you are playing volleyball at the beach. You find a beautiful, complicated watch in the sand. It has all kinds of dials, hands, and little windows on the face. It has buttons on the side. When you open the back and look inside, you see all kinds of levers, gears, little weights, and even a battery filling up the limited space. What would you guess?"

"I would guess someone lost it. It looks expensive."

The Man was patient and waited for the boy.

"The windows, dials, buttons, and hands keep track of seconds, hours, days, nights, months, years … and the sun, moon, astral signs, and other stuff," the boy continued.

The Man responded, "Good answer!"

Dialogue Thirteen
The Watchmaker

The Man opened His Bible to Matthew 7:15–16.[15] He offered the Bible to the boy and made an open palm gesture with his hand, indicating that the boy should start reading. The Man displayed approval as the boy accepted the Bible.

The boy puffed himself up, as he was getting more and more of a thrill reading aloud to The Man. He was gaining in confidence. He dreamed that he would one day know many different languages. Especially the ones where he could talk to girls romantically. "Beware of false prophets who come to you disguised as sheep but underneath are ravenous wolves. You will be able to tell them by their fruits. Can people pick grapes from thorns or figs from thistles?"

The Man stopped him from reading and spoke: "What if I told you that I was the watchmaker? Do you think I am a false prophet?"

"Oh, wow!" said the boy. "What's a watchmaker got to do with being a false prophet?"

The Man smiled with that mysterious twinkle. "Tell me what you think about a watchmaker."

The boy felt proud as he responded. "You have to be smart to know how to get all the parts to work together in such a small space. The shiny, silvery stuff looks like it would last a long time. It's polished or made of stuff that won't rust. It looks like it's automatic and doesn't need winding. I bet it's really accurate."

"What kind of person is a watchmaker?" The Man asked.

The boy answered, "It takes a lot of planning, a lot of engineering skills, and science know-how to make a watch. I would even guess that you knew how to work on many different machines to make all the little parts. Did you make each part or did you—what do you call it?—mass-produce them?"

The Man did not respond to the boy's questions. He was directing the boy to profound conclusions. "In the Bible, the sun, moon, and stars are created on the fourth day.[16] What does that tell you about the planning and accuracy of the good deeds of the first three days, if there are twenty-four-hour Earth days?"

"Ah, I don't know, maybe you were just beginning to make the parts and put them together in the right way. Maybe they weren't accurate enough and needed some fine-tuning," The boy continued, speaking his thoughts. "Twenty-four-hour days probably didn't exist, because the earth takes twenty-four hours to rotate on its axis. The earth can't rotate if it didn't exist until the fourth day."

The Man was joyful over the boy's progress. The boy was gaining in confidence. His self-respect and self-esteem were beginning to show. He did not doubt or defend himself as often. His fear of being whipped or beaten by the strop was almost gone.

The Man knew there would always be remnants of the past pains in the boy's thoughts. Abuse was like a retched boil that had to be lanced. Once you got to the core, some healing could occur. The boy still did not know how to forgive himself or others. However, he would learn. At seventeen, his work ethic was good. The Man was happy and He praised the boy. "You have a sharp mind. I like your logic. Logic is a way of thinking, and it has its own set of rules as a language. Do you remember the discussion we had about mourning?"

"Yeah, I learned about my ability to mourn the death of old ways, old traditions, or outdated laws. Mourning brings happy tears to my eyes, as I understood new laws and new concepts. I mourn the old that brings on the new. But I still don't understand the details in the arrow of time. It's Einstein's ideas about relativity, and time shortening as you approach the speed of light, that I have a hard time understanding.

"Do you know the fairy tale about Humpty Dumpty?" The twinkle in The Man's eyes exposed His inescapable charisma.

The boy became overly excited. He started laughing as he repeated the rhythmic-sounding words: "Yeah, Humpty Dumpty sat on a wall; Humpty Dumpty had a great fall. All the king's horses and all the king's men couldn't put Humpty Dumpty together again. Once Humpty, the egg, was scrambled, he could never again be unscrambled."

"Very good!" said The Man. "Humpty Dumpty is an allegory for the arrow of time. The past is over. The instant of the present is here and gone and leads into the future. The arrow of time passes."

Dialogue Fourteen
The Nobel Prize–Winning Scientist

The boy listened with his whole being, and then spoke with words of wisdom. In this way, he was like a child of God, who could solve riddles. "I understand! Humpty Dumpty represents the arrow of time! Humpty was on the wall. He fell. He broke apart and was scrambled. All the king's men and horses couldn't put him together again, no matter how important they were, or how powerful or skilled. The arrow of time flies by."

The Man interjected, "The arrow of time goes from order to disorder.[17] Unless, of course, one puts in a lot of work keeping things in order."

The boy's happiness was evident. "Yeah! Humpty Dumpty was a live egg with all his parts together in all the right places inside his shell, just like the watch. After falling, his shell smashed to smithereens, and his guts spread all over the ground. Hey, I can mourn and cry for Humpty Dumpty dying, but where are the happy tears? What do I learn from his dying?"

The Man responded. "You learn that tears come with love. You bless Humpty Dumpty. Just like at the dinner table you bless the food."

The boy watched The Man smiled again, and his eyes twinkled in that captivating way of his. "What happens to a scrambled egg? Think about it." The Man had answered his question with a question. The Man didn't make him feel guilty, stupid, or self-conscious.

"We eat it!" the boy yelled with glee. "When things die, others eat them to keep up their energy."

The Man said, "You got it."

A newfound energy swept through the boy. "That's how others grow into something more orderly and older, say, like a cow. We feed it until it is ready to become food for us. We then kill it and eat it. When living things are young, growing, and healthy, they are orderly. As they get older, they quit growing, get unhealthy, and become disorderly. They die and become food for other living things.

The Man then introduced into their discussion a Nobel Prize–winning scientist in chemistry. "Professor Ilya Prigogine[18] explained the arrow of time as going from certainty to uncertainty, from order to disorder."

"Well," the boy said, "Humpty Dumpty was certainly a live whole egg; then he went to being the uncertainty of a whole egg."

The Man rolled his eyes at the boy. "Your words are essentially correct, but twisted. We can believe the professor's words as a scientist who seeks the truth through experimentation. We can also believe his words as if he were a prophet. He is not a wolf in sheep's clothing."

Dialogue Fifteen
The Medium

"Are you okay with using the ideas of a Nobel Prize winner?" asked The Man.

The boy answered, "I guess we can believe his words. He must be really smart to get the Nobel Prize."

The Man said, "Being smart is not the number one priority for winning the Nobel Prize. Many people are smarter than some Nobel Prize winners.

"To win the prize is to find the right new language for an idea, experiment, a new theory, or other things worthy of praise. Prizewinners help people in two ways to become the children of God, whether they know it or not. One is by hard work and patience. Two is by giving the world something new to think about. They think outside the box. The idea and language of their prize contributes to the evolution of humans to be more like God. The prizewinners are somewhat like the prophets of God."

The Man continued. "Asking what you would call stupid questions and seeking their answers is what Professor Ilya does. He asked, 'Did time start with the big bang?'[19] His questions, like yours, are profound. Two other questions he queried: 'What are the roots of time?' and 'Did time preexist our universe?'

"Professor Ilya proposed an answer to the big bang using chaos theory. He said, 'Instability within a medium produced the big bang of our universe. The big bang marked the start of matter, and the start of an arrow of time. Although the matter of our universe has an age, something has no age.[20]

"In addition let me say, that this something produced the medium that became matter."

The boy started to interrupt, but The Man suddenly raised his hand. "Let's stop and listen with our hearts, souls, and minds to what the professor is saying."

After a couple of minutes, the boy shouted in ecstasy. "Oh, I get it! I'm imagining a picture in my head of a sorcerer looking at his big empty cauldron. He looks confused, trying to think of what to put in it.

He watches as his magic starts to fill the cauldron with a silvery, shiny, sparkling substance. The silvery substance forms into tiny volcanoes with wires sticking out the top, forming the backside of a circuit board. On the other side are the resistors, capacitors, transistors, and other parts needed to fit with other circuit boards to make a computer. The medium was a super-duper computer."

The Man looked at the boy with wonder and admiration. His love swelled as He hugged the boy to his chest. The boy was coming close to being a child of God. "Well, let's be careful with exaggerated fables. Yes, I know that I used parables to teach truths and morals. However, comparing the Father to a magical sorcerer as an enchanter exercising supernatural powers may push the envelope. Let us make sure the fable has no evil spirits. Do continue with your epiphany of an imaginary fable."

The boy beamed with joy and pleasure. "Okay, the sorcerer is trying to be like God. The silvery, shiny, sparkling substance is a computer that has not been born yet, so it has no age. Nevertheless, God made it. God always is, so He does not have to be born, so He has no age. God turns on the computer, programs it to stir a medium, and creates a swirling within the medium, like a hurricane or a tornado or something like the new idea of chaos theory.[21] This produces the big bang of our universe.

"It marks the start of matter, and the beginning of an arrow of time, but not the start of time. Although the matter of our universe has an age with an arrow of time, God as Time has no age, no beginning, and no end. Matter started aging as the arrow of time began at the big bang. God is so cool!"

The boy could hardly believe he had used that many words.

CHAPTER FOUR
A seventeen–then eighteen-year-old boy learns about God

Dialogue Sixteen
The Deist

The Man looked at the boy with an overabundance of love. He asked, "Do you really believe in God? Do you really believe that God is cool?"

"Yeah, you really are a good teacher, and I am learning to understand Your words. You don't put me down or talk trash. You don't make me feel stupid. I'm beginning to understand." He paused. "In my heart, I know you are gentle, and I feel your kindness."

"Thank you!" The Man replied. "That is the nicest thing you have said to me." The Man quickly raised his hands above His head and clapped. "Let's play a game. Since I know that all things are possible with the Father, I'm going to allow you to play a betting game.

"Blaise Pascal[22], a French philosopher, mathematician, and physicist of the sixteen hundreds, made a wager and he called it 'hedging your bets.' Pascal said, 'If you bet there *isn't* a God, and you get to heaven only to find out there *is* a God, then you have lost the big happening of eternal bliss.'"[22]

The Man paused for effect. "'If you bet there *is* a God, and there *isn't* at the end, it's not such a big deal.' What is the better strategy?"

The boy answered quickly. "So I bet that there is a God. Okay?"

The Man asked, "Do you mind if we talk about God, now that you are sure you will bet on Him?"

"Yeah, let's talk about Him!" said the boy.

"Do you know the difference between a deist and a theist?"

The boy looked at The Man as though he was crazy. How could He ask such a question? Then he thought of the questions he asked. He felt good being with The Man. He could feel love coming from The Man. The Man was again challenging his hunger and thirst for righteousness and enlightenment. He was again pushing the boy to search for something great. However, the boy again became defensive. "What's this, some more dumb word games?" However hard the boy tried to be something else, his sarcastic demeanor always rose like sour spit in his mouth. His abuse still lingered, so he became the abuser.

The Man smiled.

The boy felt remorse. He knew in his heart The Man's answer. He tried to remember all that he had learned. *God as Time has no age; I am! I am the Word! I am the Logos! I am Time! Humpty Dumpty represents the arrow of time. I am the watchmaker; the arrow of time is an illusion. The Father created the medium. It is full of languages, pure mathematics, and energy.* The boy tried to be contrite.

"So I gambled on there being a God, and now I have to know whether he's a deist or a theist? Will I have to choose whether He's a deist and/or a theist?

"Maybe," said The Man. I will explain the two, and then you can choose. If you want to make a choice."

The Man spoke in a voice so eloquent and with such a cadence that the words totally captured the boy. "A deist is one who believes in the existence of a God on the evidence of reason and nature only. He rejects supernatural revelation." The Man put his index finger to His lips for attention and silence. "He believes in a God who created the world but has since remained indifferent to his creation."

The boy interrupted anyway. No matter how he tried, his attention span was only so long. "Are you almost through?"

"Yes, just a few more words. His God does not need to communicate with people. The deist God is like the watchmaker who has no concern about losing his watch in the sand. A person who believes in deism behaves as a humanist. He does not need God to exist; he can do all things possible by himself as a human."

The boy's eyes started to roll and wander.

"To a deist, God is an inventor of mathematics and physics and the natural laws of the universe.

"Wait, let me think!" said the boy. "My dad used to say that mathematicians and physicists were eggheads who went to Harvard and couldn't tell the working man the time of day. To him, this deist God is not concerned with the common man. I know you've been really nice to me, and the way I think is kind of dumb. So, my dad must be wrong. You can't be an abuser." The boy knew in his heart that abuse and violence were wrong. "I'll try to pay attention."

The Man sat silent for a few minutes and let the boy gather himself. Then He continued. "Well, anyway, the deist's God started the universe in motion about fourteen billion years ago, and then wandered off to deal with other more important matters.

"Einstein thought of God this way. He thought that God did not play dice with the universe. Einstein was a determinist, and he thought God was a determinist. God determined the universe to be and then let it be. Einstein's equation showed that the curvature of space causes matter to move and matter causes space to curve. His is a determinist's universe."[23]

"Okay … I kinda understand this kind of God. My dad was like that. He would get drunk and wander away. His only concern was his next bottle of wine."

Dialogue Seventeen
The Theist

Promising himself he would pay attention, the boy asked, "Okay, what's a theist?"

The Man replied, "A theist is one who believes in one God as the Creator and ruler of the universe. A theist believes that God communicates with his creation. A theist's God does not reject supernatural revelation. He likes to reveal himself and his will to his creatures with unconditional love."

"Wait," interrupted the boy. "Slow down. If God is Time, then he can talk to everything at the same second in the arrow of time, right? He would talk to the hearts, souls, and minds of everyone. The more you were like a child of God, the easier it would be to listen and hear His words."

The Man roared with delight! He waited until the boy's emotions settled down, then He continued. "Yes, a theist believes God desires some kind of relationship with those special creatures called human beings. He has instilled this special glimpse of himself into each one of them. This is the God of Abraham, and certainly not the god of Einstein."

After a slight pause, The Man continued. "A theist believes God has a Son in Jesus. He believes that God has a spirit in the Holy Spirit." The Man opened the Bible to Genesis Chapter 1:20–31[24] He gave the Bible to the boy. "Please? Read it silently."

The boy read in deep thought. After a few minutes, he looked up from the Bible.

The Man said, "Explain to me what you read."

Shyly, the boy spoke. "On the fifth and sixth day, God created all living things. He created swimming creatures, flying creatures, cattle, wild animals, and in his own likeness, he created man. God created man in His image. It was all good."

"That was a good summary. Do you think you deserve a high grade?"

"Oh, yeah!" replied the boy.

"You do deserve a high grade, because I know you carefully read the chapter in Genesis. You should now begin to understand the wisdom of God. God did not tell Moses everything. What God left out of the book of Genesis by not telling Moses was the mathematical languages.

"He didn't tell Moses about pure energy. He was saving the languages of DNA and other mathematical languages in the medium for a later moment in the arrow of time. At the time of Moses, it was more important for him to know and spread the moral laws in one literary or learned language."

"Whoa!" exclaimed the boy. A look of confusion and bewilderment was on his face. "What about the Tower of Babel? I thought God wanted many languages. And besides, what's all this mumbo jumbo got to do with the price of beans?—as my ole Daddy would say."

The Man chuckled. "For modern-day linguistic experts, there are an estimated seven thousand vernacular languages spoken around the world. Each species is to have its own hereditary code of life written in its DNA. Each species will have some means of communication.

"If we jump to the year two thousand, the press and TV media trumpeted that the first draft of the human genome—the DNA of the human species—had its own instruction book assembled. President Bill Clinton said that without a doubt, 'it was the most important, most wondrous map ever produced by humankind.' Today, we are learning the language in which God created life. We are gaining ever more awe for the complexity, the beauty, and the wonder of God's most divine and sacred gift.

"Rigorously trained scientist Francis S. Collins, leader of the international Human Genome Project, endorsed the president's words with his own. 'It's a happy day for the world. It is humbling and awe-inspiring for me to realize that we have caught the first glimpse of our own instruction book, previously known only to God.'"[25]

The Man continued, saying, "The Father began the Kingdom of God with love. His love is His Time. The 'price of beans' is what has come into being after the Kingdom was life on the earth with the simple instructions: Do unto others, as you would have others do unto you. God gave His love, His Time. Defining a measure of love as an 'unto others' where God gave His Time. Creating life was an 'unto others.' Creating the scientific and natural laws of heaven and Earth was an 'unto others.' Our medium for languages was becoming quite extensive as an 'unto others.' The wisdom of God to give each species a way of communicating, this was an 'unto others.' The Father will continue to contribute His Time through supernatural revelation as an 'unto others.' The languages of the moral laws are yet to come. These will be love, the measure of the 'unto others.'"[25]

Dialogue Eighteen
I Am the Word! I Am the Logos! I Am Time!

"Do you remember when you gambled on there being a God?" The Man asked tenderly.

"Yeah," replied the boy.

"Do you also remember when you asked the question?" he continued in a loving tone.

The boy replied, "Do I have to know whether he's a deist or a theist? I also asked, 'Will I have to choose whether he's a deist or a theist?' The boy scoffed slightly. "Yeah, well, I remember all that." The boy was befuddled. He liked to be the one in control and ask questions. He became defensive when he had to answer questions.

"What's wrong with my words?"

After a few moments of silence, the boy replied, "Sure, I remember I said those words, and I absolutely bet there is a God. What's it to ya!" As soon as he spoke, he was ashamed and sorry for his words. The boy bowed his head; he felt remorse for being a smart aleck. He pondered what The Man was thinking. The boy was learning to think more and more like The Man.

He said to The Man. "You know, I am really getting to trust you." He waited, then continued. "So, yeah, I see what you are getting at. Now that I know the descriptions, I would say that I like God more as a theist. He could be a deist, but that's too much like my dad. But my bet is, there is a God."

"So you believe Him to behave in a stereotypical way, like a theist rather then a deist?" The Man questioned kindly.

The boy looked puzzled. "What's stereotypical?"

The Man answered. "A person who is like everybody else; he uses what we call conventional everyday wisdom. The worst case would be that he is biased, bigoted, or prejudiced…with a narrow mind I think the word prejudice fits you the best of the three."

The boy gulped and almost swallowed his tongue. "You think that's me?" He waited for an answer. Getting none, he proceeded. "That's more like my dad. He's bigoted and prejudiced!"

The Man smiled.

The boy felt in his heart and soul The Man's answer. "Now that you made me think, I think God is neither a theist nor a deist." The boy tried to sneak this in and play both sides.

All of a sudden, he heard words echoing in his heart and through his whole body. He couldn't believe what was going on in his head! Was he going crazy? The words he was hearing were melodic, soothing, and soft in tone, yet loud enough to hear. They were not forceful. They were alluring, peaceful phrases pulling him into joy. He realized the joy was a state of "in the now."

I am! I am the Word! I am the Logos! I have no beginning or end. I am Time! I have no age! I can communicate with everything at the same instant in the arrow of time. I can talk to the heart, soul, and mind of everyone.

A theist believes I am the Creator and ruler of the universe. He believes I communicate with my creation. I am also the watchmaker; the arrow of time is an illusion. My domain is in the spiritual world. A realm examined with the heart, soul, and mind. A state of "in the now."

I created and programmed the medium. It is full of languages, mathematics, and pure energy. The mathematical languages and solutions depend on the utmost accuracy. I created the medium for sharing languages. It is full of common everyday languages.

The truth is in the medium. Humans have the proper gifts to dwell in the medium and learn all the languages. The ability to find solutions to the more difficult mathematical problems depends on how the children of God increase their computing power.

We—the Father, Son, and the Holy Spirit—stirred the medium over fourteen billion years ago in Earth time. The medium holds the answers. We programmed instability within the medium and produced the big bang of the universe. The arrow of time started with the big bang. Humpty Dumpty is an allegory for the arrow of time. The matter of the universe began to have an age. The arrow of time passes. The past is over. The instant of the present is here and gone ... and leads into the future.

Dialogue Nineteen
A Singularity![26]

The Man was speaking to him. The boy came out of his reverie.

"At the beginning moment of the big bang, do you think you understand the same purpose for the medium as the Father, Son, and Holy Spirit?"

"Huh? I don't know. I don't have the foggiest clue." His mind was still a little cloudy from hearing the voice of the Father.

"This might be the most difficult part of your learning. Do you feel you can continue?"

"Yeah, I think so." The Man watched the boy's body language for a moment and then continued. "The medium is called a singularity by scientists."

The boy, always thinking he was witty, and trying to wake up, said, "What's that, a single in baseball?"

The Man looked at the boy with a half smile on his face. "Most of the time in our conversations, you can be quite amusing. Now, at this moment …" The Man slowly waved his hand back and forth. "You are about half-amusing."

Like an immature brat, the seventeen-year-old boy pouted, yet he realized the fairness in the discipline. He contritely said, "I'm sorry."

The Man accepted the apology. The boy could feel the warmth and love from The Man.

In the most wonderful and encouraging voice, The Man said, "A singularity is something totally extraordinary. It is remarkable in its unusual way. It is unique. It is a point, like in all geometries, that has no dimensions in space or time. It exists in our thoughts. It existed in God's thoughts. Do you understand so far?"

The boy was still foggy. He was completely dumbfounded, his brain almost on overload. "I don't know! I can't get any kind of picture of what it is. It just seems like it is nothing."

The Man scolded him. "You have to use all your abilities as a child of God to understand. You are capable. You have to listen to your heart. Start by telling yourself that you know a singularity exists, yet you cannot touch it, see it, hear it, taste it, or smell it. You bet that God exists. 'Why are you so frightened, you who have so little faith'?"[27]

"No!" said the boy. "I believe that God exists! I have faith in Him and You!" He was loud, trying to convince himself that he truly did believe with his heart, soul, and mind. He tried to use his imagination. *He saw the Three Persons of the Trinity in his mind's eye, but he had a hard time making them into one nature.*

The Man spoke assertively. "Then call forth who you are! Call forth your beatitudes.[28] Call forth the code of who you are that is imprinted in your DNA. God gave you gifts of courage, intelligence, and sensitivity. Call them forth."

The boy felt cold chills all over his body. He was shaking. He had never experienced this kind of fright before. He was so scared he thought he was going to wet his pants. Even when his father beat him, he felt pain and rejection more than fear.

The Man reached out and embraced the boy. The boy felt the surge of warmth and safety. He would be an immature eighteen-year-old in a month, but he still needed hugs. The Man cuddled him until the shaking stopped. Then He held him out and looked in the boy's eyes. The boy looked back and made eye contact. The boy saw the compassion and concern in The Man's eyes. His tears started to flow. The boy couldn't stop sobbing deep within himself. The Man took the knuckle of his index finger and wiped a tear away. He said, "I am going to save this tear forever as a sign of our love. It will be an 'unto others.'

"Just feel the love we have shared in these discussions, little big man. Keep your hopes up, and above all, have faith. The Father will help you understand your purpose." The Man waited for the boy to calm down. Then He gently spoke to the boy in a soft, soothing tone, Man to man.

"Let us continue. Just think of your crying as the big bang. All of a sudden, your tears burst forth, yet you do not know from where or why they came. The medium is a singularity that bursts forth as the big bang, yet you do not know from where or why it came. Yet you can understand that these are God's messages. God exists, and

He created the medium as a singularity. You know this by faith as a spiritual truth.

"You now know this by science, as the evidence and data the scientists have gathered has led to this theoretical truth. It is not a perfect truth; however, it is like going from Galileo to Newton to Einstein. It gets more complex as these prophets of science take languages and knowledge from the medium."

The boy interjected what he thought was a brilliant idea. "The knowledge increases and the understanding gets better. The wisdom of it all is just over the horizon. I should ask for wisdom like Solomon." The boy suddenly felt overwhelmed with humility. He realized for the first time in his life that faith in God made him humble. Being a smart aleck was a thing of the past. There was so much to learn. He said to the Man, "I do believe in God, and I believe in his medium as a singularity. It is His single source of love. Are You and the Father and the Holy Spirit a singularity? Am I going to learn more about a singularity?"

Dialogue Twenty
Toy Boats, Chaos, Universal Constants

"When am I going to learn more about a singularity?" the boy asked. He was sitting on the mulch in a yoga position.

The Man was beaming with joy. "Right now!"

The boy was ecstatic as The Man started explaining more about a singularity.

"It is extremely sensitive to initial conditions. If you change the initial state by a tiny amount, it changes its future significantly. It is chaotic."

The Man looked down at the boy as He sat on the rock. The Man smiled with that warm twinkle in his eyes. "Can you think of a situation like Humpty Dumpty's?"

"What do you mean?" The boy pondered the question. After a few minutes, he responded, "How about a boat? Will it solve the riddle?"

"What about a boat?" The Man answered with a question. He wanted the boy to think.

"Let me see," said the boy, concentrating. He stuck his fist under his chin and leaned his elbow on his thigh. He portrayed the image of *The Thinker*—the sculpture by Auguste Rodin. "I have a picture in my head. You did say to use my imagination. There are these two toy boats. I'll put them in a flowing creek, one after the other. I'll run down the side of the creek, watching the two boats. They don't follow the same path. They zigzag differently, depending on the flow of the water. Since the water is flowing, it has little eddies and whirlpools that change the direction of the boats. After a while, the boats are moving differently but still going down with the stream's flow."

"So what is the point?" The Man asked.

"It's a perfect—what's the word you'd use?—*parable?* No, an allegory," the boy answered.

"You put the boats in the water at two different times. Or even in two different places. This changes the initial state by a tiny amount. The boats' future movements were changed significantly as they moved down the stream. It is chaotic. You can't predict the exact path of either boat."

The Man marveled at the imagination, creativity, and intelligence of the boy. He would find ways to stimulate his hunger and thirst for righteousness, his search for something great. He would encourage learning the beatitudes in depth so he could understand his gifts. The Man would find ways to challenge the boy to have fun and enjoy the little eddies and whirlpools in the path of his life. He would teach him how to handle the problems of his trials and tribulations with a positive attitude. The will of the Father would help him grow in all ways.

The Man continued His teaching. "Are you ready to continue now that you have an idea of chaos?"

"Yeah, let's get it on!" He reached up to give The Man a high five.

The Man ignored his enthusiasm and just focused on chaos. "Well, we created the medium as a singularity. We kept it stable, in its initial condition, until we had it full of all the languages that humans would need through their evolution.

"The languages in the medium would describe all past and future systems of the universe. There were alphabets and words for all the vernacular languages. There were numbers, shapes, and equations for all the mathematics. This included two of the most famous numbers: $Pi = \pi$ ... and the natural logarithm e. Notice that their decimals carry on forever without repeating a pattern." These numbers delighted The Man.

"Pi and e are irrational numbers that are universal constants that never change. Universal constants are like the water for your toy boats. Water is water and never changes. The state of the water can change from a solid—ice—to a liquid and to a gas—steam. The water can flow and move, but it stays at the molecular level as H_2O, a constant.

"Pi stays as pi. However, when you multiply it by r^2, the radius of a circle, the product equals the   area of a circle. A basic example of how a constant works is $\pi r^2 = a$. What would happen if we did change the constants?" The Man proceeded to answer His own question.

"If we changed any of these constants, a tiny amount in the initial state of the medium, it would change all the future energies in the universe. We would have a completely different universe. A circle would no longer look like a circle. This is the concept of chaos."[29]

Dialogue Twenty-One
A Very Confused boy

The Man repeated the last three thoughts because of their importance in establishing the universe. "Remember, if we changed any of these constants, a tiny amount in the initial state of the medium, it would change all the future energies in the universe. We would have a completely different universe. Circles would look different. The shape of the moon and Earth would be different. This is the concept of chaos."

While The Man was reiterating these thoughts, the boy was staring at him as if he were an apparition. When The Man finished, the boy asked in a most sardonic manner, "Why did you repeat those results? Whoopee! What's the purpose?"

With all the patience in heaven and on Earth, The Man responded calmly. "The purpose of the constants is to fine-tune the universe as it now exists." With the utmost control, The Man asked gently, "Who is going to benefit from the constants in the medium?"

The boy was still unsettled. He hesitated before he answered in a befuddled and shamed manner. "People, I guess!"

"Fairly good answer. Now that you know the purpose and who is going to benefit, it is up to you to learn as much as you can about the features of the medium." The Man reflected aloud. "This is Our will."

The boy now understood this concept in his heart, mind, and soul.

The Man proceeded further. "The mathematics in the medium will describe all the energies in the universe. For example, Einstein's equation, E equals mc^2, explains how energy is converted into mass, and mass is converted into energy."[30]

"Hold your horses, Buster Brown," the boy interjected. He immediately realized his lack of manners. "Oops, I'm sorry. The words just jumped out." The boy paused before continuing. "We go from a singularity to the medium, to chaos, to languages, to alphabets, to numbers, to equations, to energies, to what is next."

The Man replied lovingly, "To the most wonderful concept of all: the constancy of the speed of light.[31] In the 1870s, James Clerk

Maxwell[32] established the speed of light as a physical constant of the universe that cannot be changed or exceeded without changing the universe. He was a friend of Charles Dodson, a shy young mathematics teacher. Dodson wrote *Alice's Adventures in Wonderland* and *Through the Looking Glass.* He wrote under the pen name of Lewis Carroll to a young girl named Alice. The stories were allegories and metaphors about the mathematics and physics of Maxwell."

The boy was amazed. He'd thought *Alice* was for girls. Being eighteen, he would read it to get rid of his bias.

"The initial state of the universe will come from the pure energy of the medium. The energies will develop into many forms—all described by one language or another, depending on the speed of light. Einstein established the speed of light and inertial systems as axioms as they are expressed in the special theory of relativity."[33]

The Man adjusted His speaking tone and volume from that of a forgiving, loving teacher to one of a loving father. "Hey, I see that you have your ball and glove. You want to play catch as we talk?"

The boy jumped up and ran twenty paces, counting them off as he ran. He made a pitcher's mound with his foot. He leaned over like a pitcher looking for his sign. He waited for The Man to get down in His catcher's crouch to give the sign. The Man put down one finger for a fastball. The boy did his windup and delivered his best fastball.

"Strike one," The Man hollered.

The boy continued to pitch as The Man called out balls and strikes. He was also persistent in giving his lecture about languages and systems. "Vernacular languages can vary, and there can be many. Mathematical systems vary and there can be many. There are many moral systems. Interpreting and comparing the moral laws of many religions can be frustrating. Abiding by any one set of them is most difficult. The moral systems and the scientific systems must develop in harmony. Each system has its own set of rules. Abuse happens when a set of rules is forced on someone."

Full of himself, as if he were now an authority, the boy interrupted. "I remember that a foolish faith in authority is the worst enemy of truth. Here comes a curve." Deep inside his heart and soul, he felt his own hypocrisy. It didn't register in his conscious mind. The boy, unremitting, did his windup. He threw his curve. He grunted his words. "That's why God confuses humans with many languages. The people tried to build the Tower of Babel with one language spoken by all. But God can't let that happen."

Now realizing he also had a hypocritical tone, the boy walked slowly to The Man. The Man stayed in his catcher's crouch. The boy kneeled by his side. His buttocks relaxed easily on his heels. His chin almost touched his chest. He appeared to go into deep thought, as in prayer. What a quick turnaround in behavior. The boy gave the impression of being comfortable, so The Man put his arm around the boy and whispered in his ear.

"I want you to memorize and learn three *omni* words and one *bene* word."

The boy's eyes popped open. A startled look appeared on his face.

Dialogue Twenty-Two
Three Omni Words and One Bene Word

It had been awhile since their last Dialogue. The Man repeated the last thoughts of their Dialogue from six months earlier. "I want you to memorize and learn three *omni* words and one *bene* word." The Man remembered the startled look on the boy's face. A more confident look appeared on his face this time.

"Let's go for a run. We can talk as we run. We need to include our bodies with our hearts, minds, and souls." The Man smiled, pleased with getting the boy's attention. They ran.

The Man started the chat. "The first *omni* word is *omniscient*. It means infinite knowledge. It is what is in the medium. God knows all things. He put all His knowledge in the medium for humans to learn."

The boy nodded his head in understanding. He was trying to form a good attitude. The more he learned, the easier it was to understand the forms of abuse. He had to learn everything he could, to help himself and to help others. Their breathing had changed only a little as they ran. They were in good physical shape.

They still carried on their chat. "The second *omni* word is *omnipresent*. It means that God is everywhere at the same time. He is Time. So being present in the arrow of time is not a problem. He is 'in the now'! We discussed His love as His Time, where 'unto others' measures love. Ordinary time is measured by our lifetimes in seconds, hours, days, months and years. The arrow of time is a measure of time from the big bang. It is illusionary through the transfers of energy by order and disorder, certainty and uncertainty, and the making of calendars. 'In the now' is a moment of ecstasy, an epiphany, an emotional, physical or intellectual enlightenment, or an emotional orgasm or excitement."

The boy nodded his head in agreement. He had faith that The Man would be there for him in the now and in the future. The concepts of time were finally sinking into his intellect and emotions.

"The third *omni* word is *omnipotent*. It means that God is almighty, infinite in power, all-powerful, invincible, unstoppable, and supreme. He stirred the medium, and the universe began."

The boy nodded his head a third time. The Man would forever be in his heart, mind, and soul. He would be a little child to The Man.

"The *bene* word is *benevolent* or *beneficent*. It means goodness, kindness, charity, conferring benefits, and doing well consistently."

The boy opened his mouth to say something, but then thought better of it and kept quiet. He sensed a contradiction in an omniscient, omnipresent, omnipotent, beneficent God. However, The Man was persistent.

"Using the meanings of the three *omni* and one *bene* words, we can reduce the confusion and begin to understand more fully the works of God. We can clarify the Will of God."

The boy then remembered asking about the devil doing all those bad things. *Why didn't God just stop him? Why not just zap us and make us good? Wouldn't that be the works and will of God?* For once, he didn't interrupt The Man. He'd ask later. His concentration reverted to The Man.

They continued running. "These are His works. The constants during the big bang, and after in the arrow of time, gave the universe stability. They determined the flow of energies throughout the universe." The Man was speaking slowly, as if reminiscing and loving every thought that was going into the boy's heart, mind, and soul. "There are fifteen constants[34], like Pi, *e*, and *c*, that cannot vary. The speed of light is a constant. The constants were present at the beginning of the big bang. They determined the states and properties of the universe. They gave stability to a somewhat chaotic universe."[35]

The man knew he had to get the boy's undivided attention. He startled the boy by saying, "Don't forget Mrs. Andrews's 'answer': 'Just do it, because I'm the teacher and I'm telling you so.'"

The boy made a funny face at The Man.

The Man could feel the boy's tension rising. "The Father established the constants. They will not change. He is telling you so! He realizes your needs! I repeat, the constants give the universe stability.

"People require accurate standards for measurements in mass, length, and time to understand their immediate world and the universe. Having an 'unto others' to measure love will build self-esteem. The consistency is good. Feeling secure satisfies a basic need.

The phenomenal use of numbers is good. Humans can celebrate the creation of the real numbers."

Dialogue Twenty-Three
Rules of Law

They kept running, but The Man paused in his chat. He and the boy were in deep thought. After a while, The Man spoke as if in a dream. "A complete theory of quadratic equations requires the introduction of the imaginary unit, square root of negative one, and the complex numbers for solutions. All these languages are stored in the medium. It is good." The Man repeated the sequence of the medium.

"God stirred the medium and created a swirling within the medium, like a hurricane or a tornado or something like the mathematics of chaos would describe. This produced the big bang of our universe. The big bang marks the start of matter, and the beginning of an arrow of time[36], in earth time, but not the start of God or I am He[37] Time.

"The arrow of time as we humans know it is a dimension. A second is the dimensional measure of time. Length is a dimension. An inch measures a length. The universe can be measured in terms of mass, length and time. In Einstein's theory of relativity, mass, length and time warp as one approaches the speed of light.

"God is Time. The Father began the Kingdom with love. The Kingdom is beyond how we measure the universe. So God as Time is measured in love. As We said before, we can measure love in 'unto others'. How many or how much 'unto others' did you do today?"

The Man's enthusiasm was infectious. The boy came out of his reverie with eagerness. He ran backward as he turned to face The Man. He started talking excitedly about the words and concepts he had learned.

"The matter of our universe has an age with the arrow of time; God as Time has no age—no beginning and no end. He is now. He is omnipresent." He paused and gave an impish smile. "Matter started aging as the arrow of time began at the big bang. God is omnipotent. He is infinite in power. The truth is in the medium. It is full of languages. God is omniscient. He has infinite knowledge."

The Man interrupted. "Didn't you say God is so cool? What do you think the Father had in the medium at the beginning moment of the big bang?"

The boy was reluctant to answer. The Man took a different tact. "Do you remember the answer to the question?"

"Yeah, I kinda remember," said the boy. "Wasn't it pure energy and languages programmed on the circuit boards of a powerful computer?"

"You have a good memory. Can you describe what happened?"

The boy was anxious and reluctant to answer. "Well, I guess the energy turned into matter. I really don't know what happened to the languages. Would they still be stored in the medium?"

The Man answered, "Yes, that is a brilliant insight. The medium will be available for humans to learn everyday languages, all the learned languages, all of literature and mathematics."

The boy started another discussion by wondering aloud. "How do you learn the languages in the medium?"

The Man answered, "Yes, again that is a brilliant question. Humans must work hard and search for new phases of knowledge. Increasing their knowledge of the moral and social laws will be a benefit to their ability of loving 'unto others.' Natural and scientific laws are consistent and in harmony for their own evolution. The medium will be available for humans to learn the languages required for their growth to attain and give love 'unto others.'

"Each culture and its society will have its own everyday language, dialect, and vernacular stored in the medium. Common everyday languages can vary. There can be many dialects and vernacular languages. Literary or learned languages are many and varied. However, let us repeat the sad commentary to the estimated seven thousand languages spoken around the world. One language dies out about every two weeks, according to linguistic experts struggling to save at least some of them."[38]

The boy interrupted, as was his style. At eighteen, he still wanted people to feel sorry for him. "Boy, there you go again, using big ideas I don't know! What am I going to do? I guess I'll have to learn to use a wordbook, a dictionary. I'll have to learn how to read."

The boy was so phony in his simple naiveté that The Man laughed at his faked seriousness. Again, The Man felt the need to discipline the boy. The Man explained. "Playing by a set of rules is restrictive.

Reading, interpreting the meaning, and learning the language of different cultures can be frustrating. Abiding by the moral laws of each society's rules of law is difficult. We gave Moses the languages required for the moral laws. The people felt the laws and rules were being forced on them, so they rebelled."

They had stopped running. They walked into the shade of their little umbrella of trees. The Man sat on his rock. The boy sat on his haunches. He became his true self, a child of God. He started laughing aloud. He couldn't stop. He giggled the words out as he was laughing. He was on an adrenaline rush.

"Boy, I would never wish to be a Sadducee or a Pharisee, that's for sure. I would never be a lawyer or a preacher. They are so smooth with words. I can just see me, a pimple-faced teenager in a Roman toga, arguing a case before the Sanhedrin or the Supreme Court. Yeah! Wearing a toga at the Supreme Court is a scream. He stood up, acting as if he were modeling. He acted as if he were flipping a fold of his Roman toga over his shoulder. "That's soooo funny."

The Man laughed with the boy, not at him. He knew the boy would outgrow his phony naiveté. He appreciated the moments when the boy used his imagination and was a true child of God. Innocence was not all bad. He persisted in challenging the boy's intellect. "We created the scientific and natural laws of heaven and Earth for all to use, not to confuse. Moral and scientific laws are consistent and in harmony with your own evolution. As you grow in the knowledge of different languages, you grow in the understanding of communicating with others.

"Learning about the medium is a much more thorough explanation of the creation. The initial conditions were so important for the starting of the universe with the big bang. When added to the description of Genesis, it is more than enough for an explanation of the first days. Science and religion must evolve together. Each has its own set of laws."

CHAPTER FIVE
An eighteen-year-old boy learns to be eclectic

Dialogue Twenty-Four
Learning to Let Go

The Man paused. He could see the thoughts whirling around in the boy's head. The boy was gaining in knowledge, understanding, and wisdom. He was growing beyond the conventional wisdom of common street language. The Man now challenged the boy's work ethic with words.

"You were abused badly when you were growing up, living with your family. You cannot use abuse any longer as an excuse. Let me repeat again the exact words we stated when we started our Dialogues. You were stubborn. You were full of anger and rage. You were narcissistic. You would fight, lie, steal, and cheat to get your way. You talked trash and used hurtful words. You asked questions to put others down, because you thought you were so smart.

"Now is the time to forgive. Forgive your mother, your father, and, most importantly, forgive yourself. Now is the time to remember the brutal, ugly violence for what it was. It is never a behavior to repeat. Let it all go." He began to share a story about two monks.

Once upon a time, early in the morning, the footfalls of two Buddhist monks' steps mired in mud as they walked down the path that led to their monastery a few miles away. It was the monsoon season, and the rain was pelting down, making it almost impossible to walk on the muddy path.

The two monks trudged on, and off to the side of the path, they heard someone crying over the noise of the deluge. The one good monk sloshed over to the side of the path and looked down into the creek that was filling rapidly with water. A young girl was fearfully clawing the side of the levee, trying to climb up to the path.

The good monk knelt and reached out, grabbed the young girl by the arm, and pulled her into his arms as he stood up on the path. As she was safety cradled in his arms, she explained that she was trying to get to her home, which was in the pasture on the other side of the path. The good monk carried her to the other side of the muddy path and put her down in the pasture so she could walk to her home. The good monk gently said to her, "Have no fear! Go in peace!"

He then turned back onto the path and continued trudging on to his monastery. The other monk, standing mired in mud with his mouth open, was totally astounded as he watched the events unfold. He could not believe what he was watching. He tried to catch up with the good monk. By the time the two monks reached the monastery, the other monk was exhausted, fuming, resentful, guilty, and full of remorse and shame.

He screamed at the good monk. He pointed a shaking finger at him, accusing him, blaming him, and judging him: "Do you know what you have done? You have talked to and touched a young girl. You have broken your vow of silence and chastity. I will have to report you to the Dalai Lama."

The good monk looked at the other monk and had nothing but sympathy, empathy, and love for his fellow monk. With sensitivity and great compassion, he softly spoke these words: "Are you still carrying the young girl? I quit carrying her when I let her down in the pasture."

The Man summarized. "The moral to this allegory is, how long does one hold on and carry burdens that are exhausting, accusing, blaming, and judgmental—burdens that cause one to be cruel, furious, resentful, guilty, and full of remorse and shame? Remember this allegory when you read. As an eighteen-year-old, read, learn, and change."

The Man made eye contact with the boy. With authority, he said, "Given that you realize the necessity of learning to read, you must also realize the need for mathematics. You are a perfect example of why the joy spilled over for us as we created the mathematical language in the code of the DNA[39] for all living things."

The Man turned away. He continued speaking. "The initial conditions for combined DNA are established at the instant of conception of an embryo." He glanced unobtrusively at the boy to see if he was listening. "The DNA is programmed with a process for the embryo to change and adapt in the womb to a fetus. The fetus continues to change and adapt. It prepares itself for birth. At birth, it gasps a couple of cold breaths, like gulping an icy sheet of dark, frigid air. It is alive as a human. The pain of the birth for the mother and child, and the pain of the first breaths, diminish quickly. The white light and warmth of an overly tired mother's embrace gives comfort to the newborn child. It is ready to be loved and cared for, just as it was loved and cared for in the womb.

"We cannot predict with certainty the life pattern a person should follow. Just as little eddies and whirlpools would affect the boat's path, so would nourishment and disease, love and hate, pleasure and pain, valor and terror, and many other opposites, affect a person's life … even death.

"Children of God have the responsibility for the three *omni* and one *bene* word. They must fulfill their responsibilities to the best of their ability. It is evident that the exquisite beauty of the DNA molecule has in its inherent ability the capacity to allow for change and adaptation.

"You, my little big man, are now a grown man, showing your DNA's inherent ability to change and adapt. You want to work hard on the path of your life. You want to be open to how events will change it, without becoming despondent and resentful."

Dialogue Twenty-Five
The Big Bang[40]

To sustain his listening and his attention, The Man was counting on the boy's work ethic and intelligence, so He persisted. "Therefore, the languages of mathematics will be in the medium for you and others to learn. It is fun sharing our love of the mathematical languages and how they describe the universe." The Man unexpectedly stopped talking. All was quiet.

The boy looked nonplussed. The Man was cheery inside yet appeared quite stoic on the outside. The boy had queasy feelings, but gave The Man his undivided attention. For what seemed an eternity, The Man and the boy sat in silence. Then The Man whispered, "Just think, to orchestrate a score in music is mathematical."

Suddenly, The Man jumped up. He tapped an imaginary baton upon an imaginary conductor's podium. He started waving the imaginary baton with his arms, as if he were a conductor leading a huge orchestra. His voice sounded as if He were a thousand-piece symphonic orchestra. His words were assertive, forceful, and utterly beautiful in their musical pitch. He sang in elegant tones of vibrato.

To the boy, The Man appeared as if He were a pure white light radiating to the boy's inner being. The words rushed through his body like warm, ardent air. The Man's words were lyrical as they burst forth from Him with an upbeat tempo and rhythm. He sang of the creation! His first words were the title to His symphony. The creation is the ultimate achievement of the wisdom of God.

"At the infinitesimal flash of the big bang[41], the medium was scrambled. It was no longer a singularity. The big bang wasn't really a big, loud noise. It was just a name. The big bang was the super force splitting into the four main forces that would form the universe. The forces were the gravitational, the electromagnetic, and the strong and weak forces of the nucleus. The super force could not go back to being a stable medium. Each force has its own mathematical language describing it. Someday people will discover the unifying mathematical theory of the forces.[42]

"Just keep in mind that the super force came from an infinitesimally tiny size. It started expanding at an extraordinary rate, faster than the speed of light. In less than a second, it locks in uniformity. In less than three seconds, the temperature cools. The temperature is uniform throughout the universe; the elements of hydrogen and helium form. The medium still exists by describing the forces of the universe with the arrow of time. The speed of light becomes a constant.[43]

"A background radiation throughout the universe exists as a remnant of the big bang. Many languages tried to explain the chaos. A mathematical language governs the pure energy as it formed according to the laws of thermodynamics."[44] In the following silence, The Man turned and bowed deeply to an imaginary audience.

The boy's thoughts resounded like echoes in his head: *Time by itself has no beginning and no end. It existed before the medium. The arrow of time came with the big bang. Energy flowed in the universe like the boats in the stream.* Alternatively, the boy's life flowed like a boat in the stream. At eighteen, he was growing into a child of God.

For some direction, the boy looked at The Man in awe. He saw none coming, so he said to The Man, "Why are you giving me that enigmatic, charismatic smile of yours? How's that for big words?" The boy didn't come close to matching the music of The Man, yet he was overly elated with his understanding, which gave him a sense of pride. His words and feelings were not a sinful pride, but the pride of hard work. The pride that comes when one is fulfilling his gifts.

He was learning to speak with an authority that came from within. He was learning to listen and speak from a heart that was truly in touch with his soul and mind. He was mimicking his new role model, The Man.

At that instant, the boy's face turned beet red. The goose bumps were apparent on his skin. The heat of his emotions was radiating from his body. He appeared to be in some kind of emotional state. His emotions gushed over with great excitement and confusion. He sensed the overwhelming feelings of faith, gentleness, goodness, humility, joy, love, peace, patience, and self-control. Each was a separate feeling.

Dialogue Twenty-Six
The Smug boy

At this point, the boy could only parrot The Man. He knew the words; he could speak with authority; he had the feelings; he felt different emotions; he knew how to listen—yet he remained uncomfortable with his lack of confidence. He was just mimicking The Man. He couldn't put it all together.

"You know something, mister? Your singing gave me chills and goose bumps. You made my emotions overflow with pleasure. My pride toward You must be sinful," the boy admitted.

The Man laughed uproariously! He stretched His hands and arms aloft in the air. His head tilted upward. His back arched. He held his pose. His countenance was pure with complete joy. His laughter was absolute jubilance. He prayed from His heart, "For You, Father."

The boy interrupted. The Man titled his head in annoyance as He looked down on the boy with his lips slightly puckered. His eyes squinted in a half-surly frown.

The boy was self-centered and didn't notice he'd annoyed The Man. "I've come to realize the importance of words. I've started going to a dictionary to learn all the words you use. I'm also learning that a person can talk with his or her body, like you do when you laugh.

"Having all these ways of communicating must be a goal of the Father. I'm beginning to understand God's idea for language. Going from prophet to scientist to lawyer to each person is the challenge for the children of God."

The Man was pleased with the boy's response, so he let the annoyance slide. The boy was gaining in confidence.

He continued his thought as he said, "We all speak differently. Is that what you meant when you spoke about *team*?"

The Man said, "Yes, as I said, it will be up to me as coach of the team to unify the people. We want the people to develop their gifts so they will be worthy of being on the team. God's will is for you to learn, to change, and to adapt."

The boy puffed himself up pompously and pronounced, "So God confused the language of the whole world at the Tower of Babel so you could be the coach of the team and teach us? How's this for words! To love, translate, and communicate in much different syntax is the mission of the coach." The boy paused. "What do you think of those words? Pretty nifty, huh!" The boy was on a roll.

"How about this: Love, truth, beauty, perfection, and wisdom are examples of words that require many languages to understand their meaning. They are symbols, like Logos, for a much higher meaning.

"Am I a copycat or am I learning? I wonder what Mrs. Andrews would say now? I also went to the library and looked up the universal constants. As you said, there are fifteen constants, including pi, *e*, and *c*. They cannot vary. The speed of light is constant. The constants were present at the beginning of the big bang and determined the properties of the universe.

"I now understand that constants anchor mathematical sentences with accuracy. They give the mathematical sentences power. I have doubts whether Mrs. Andrews was referring to universal constants when she chastised me. She was only exercising her power. I won't ever forget her answer.

"'Oh, Mrs. Andrews, The Man is teaching me some manners to go along with my words, so I forgive you for being a pompous prate. I hope that you will forgive me for being a sniveling snot.'" The boy thought he showed outward confidence for the first time ever. He never thought for a second that he was being smug. With the false pride of an eighteen-year-old, he intuitively felt that now was the time to confront The Man with a contradiction.

"I hope my Man will forgive me, but I sensed a contradiction in an omniscient, omnipresent, omnipotent, beneficent God."

The Man raised one eyebrow at the slang use of "my Man." He let it slide without remarking. The boy didn't notice. He kept talking to prove his point.

"I thought better of it at the time and kept quiet," the boy continued.

The Man smiled.

"But now I need to challenge your words. You said, 'These are His works.' You started with the constants at the big bang. They gave the universe stability, and you kept going on. You inferred that languages of science and religion in harmony had the power to answer many questions. He recited a list:

> Is God limited by space and time?
> Why did the universe come into being?
> What is the meaning of human existence?
> When does life begin?
> Is an embryo a person?
> Is a fetus a person?
> What happens after we die?
> Who decides what is a genetic improvement, if we try to reengineer our species?

"While I was quiet, I remembered asking you at the beginning of our Dialogues about the devil doing all those bad things. Why didn't God just stop him? Just zap us and make us good! Wouldn't that be the works of God?"

Dialogue Twenty-Seven
The boy's Challenge

The boy was challenging the Word of God. Perhaps he hadn't changed that much, after all. He still harbored the doggedness of abuse. "But isn't this omniscient, omnipresent, omnipotent, beneficent a God-thing in the Bible describing God as an omniscient, omnipresent, omnipotent—beneficent benevolent deity? Which simply means that God is all-knowing, all-present, all-powerful, and well-meaning? But does he care to stick around?" the boy questioned.

The boy almost laughed at himself for the gobbledygook of words he used. "Now that I have used all these words that sound like double-talk, the simple question is this: Isn't this a contradiction? How can God be all everything and well-meaning and still allow all the depression, despair, devastation, destruction, doubt, guilt, hatred, misery, pain, poverty, regret, remorse, sorrow, violence, war …? I could go on with all the bad things."

The boy sneered at The Man. He knew he was being bratty. "Again, is God there to help overcome the misery?"

The Man, expressing his full compassion answered, "Yes! The contradiction is with the human emotions, especially pain, fear, doubt, and guilt. Yet there are so many concerns. Man's starvation, war, sickness, violence, abuse from person-to-person, abuse by terrorism, and other butcheries are madness." His words tailed off into a quietness of no sound. But his body shuddered with his expression of grief.

The boy also felt sorrow; he wanted The Man to put into plain words an easy clarification. He waited until he thought The Man's composure was returning. He didn't realize how wrong he could be. The Man couldn't possibly lose his composure. Nevertheless, the boy brazenly tried his hardest to show that he had learned to mourn. Still, he didn't know if he believed what he was saying. He was becoming confused.

In a solemn tone of voice that still revealed his smugness and his warped imagination, the boy said, "Terrible things happen all the time in this world. Human tragedy seems like proof that God could not possibly be all-knowing, all-present, all-powerful, and well-meaning.

If He loves us and has the power to change our situation, why doesn't he prevent our emotional problems of doubt, pain, fear, guilt, and suffering? Wouldn't He want to do this?"

The Man grimaced. The boy's angry challenge tried to alter His attitude of affection. He quietly answered, "Listen to Our Words. You have free will. You can be narcissistic. You can be a hothead. You can be envious, jealous, spiteful, or lazy. You can be disrespectful even to the point of battering or raping someone. Would you want Us to prevent these behaviors associated with your emotions? Wouldn't it be better for you to learn how to deal with these aspects in your life? Wouldn't it be better if you could attain self-respect and self-esteem on your own merits?"

The boy was distraught. He strongly felt doubt. Had he overstepped his bounds? Was he asking one of those disobedient questions you just didn't ask? Was this a Mrs. Andrews kind of question and response? *Oh, what the heck!* thought the boy. *I'm in for a penny, why not for a dollar. What a dumb thought, with dumb words.*

He felt guilty. He jumped up, clenching his fists at his side. His body was rigid. He was confused. The painful feeling of fear surged up inside him. He was getting angry with himself, but he directed his anger at The Man. He challenged The Man even more with twisted words; harsh, loud tones; and a vitriolic attitude.

"Well, if God loves us, He can protect us. He would have to." The boy's logic failed him as he blurted out an incoherent phrase. "He's either three *omnis* and one *bene*—uncaring, or one *bene*—beneficent and three *omnis* powerless to help. Either way, where is He?"

The Man rose from the rock to his full height. He moved into the intimate space of the boy. He raised His hands. He gently and lovingly rested them on the boy's shoulders. He bowed his head and waited until the boy made eye contact. With a twinkling in His eyes and a voice that could charm any demon, He spoke tenderly. "I have taken you for my son. Would you believe that I love you?"

The Man caught him off guard. After a few seconds of hesitation, still rigid, he uttered faintly, "Oh, for sure." He unclenched his fists. The doubts left him. His anger subsided.

"Would you believe that I would do everything in My power to prevent pain and fear in your life?"

The boy knew he would contradict himself with his answer. He expressed a vague, self-satisfied answer that came close to being a lie, "Oh, absolutely."

"Would you believe that I would allow you to play in any rough sport like football?"

The boy expressed each phrase from a whisper to normal sound. "I think so."

"Would you believe that I would tell you to be careful and not get hurt?

The boy answered loudly in his smart-aleck tone. "Yeah! I would be surprised if you didn't have some comment and concern."

"So, as your Father, you would expect me to give you some basic, good advice and then let you go off and make your own mistakes?"

Dialogue Twenty-Eight
Words That Bind

The Man repeated his question: "So, as your Father, you would expect Me to give you some basic, good advice and then let you go off and make your own mistakes?"

"Well, I wouldn't want you bragging about me so I'd get embarrassed," the boy replied. "I also wouldn't want you harassing me, nagging me, and pampering me all the time, if that's what you mean. I'm not a little baby."

The Man said, "What if you did get hurt?"

The boy replied, "I think I could handle the little hurts. Like if I tackled someone, or if I got a bruise or a little cut. I got a lot of those from my dad. But if it was a big hurt, like spraining my ankle, or a big cut that needed stitches, I would want You there to care for me if I had to go to the hospital."

The Man smiled. "Accordingly, you think you can learn best by doing most things on your own. You think you can learn to be more careful. You would not take too big a risk or be foolish. Yeah, I can do those things! I think I am smart enough to learn how to take care of myself."

"Consequently, you know that, as your Father, I have the power to interfere in your life. You know I can prevent you from taking chances. You know I can guide you from putting yourself in painful situations. You know you should obey me in all things. However, you are telling Me to back off. You want Me to show My love by letting you have the freedom to learn from your own adventures."

The boy calmly matched The Man's smile with his own twinkling, smiling eyes and a voice that could charm his own demons. He said, "Oh, for sure! That's exactly what I want. I know all those things You could do to me and for me. However, see, I am learning to use Your words. I want You to trust me. I want You to know that I will tell You the truth. I want You to believe that I will be a team player. And I want You to know that everything I do, I do to please You and make You proud of me." Tears started to come into the boy's eyes; he didn't try to wipe them away. He was feeling happiness, and it pleased him. He liked the feeling. He was in the now.

"I will be like the little boat," he continued. "You can start me off on my journey. I will run into troubles. I want You on the bank, ready to help if I call. However, I want to steer myself through the eddies and whirlpools, the trials and tribulations."

The Man finally spoke. "Well, little man, that was quite a soliloquy. However, we must clarify two of the many questions. The first question to clarify is whether you believe that I would do everything in my power to prevent pain and fear in your life."

The boy looked at Him in astonishment. The Man had a funny little grin on his face. The grin was that of the Cheshire Cat in *Alice in Wonderland*. The Man easily saw through his hoax.

"You knew you would contradict yourself with an answer. However, you still expressed a bogus answer: 'Oh, for sure.' You came close to lying to Me. Let it be known between us," The Man said authoritatively, "that this is where I am coming from! I will tolerate no lies. I will tolerate no disrespect." He stared at the boy. "I want it to be absolutely clear that I would do everything in My power to prevent pain, fear, doubt, guilt, and suffering in your life. However, if I did, I would then be taking away your basic, strongest, real emotions and feelings. You would no longer be a child of God.

"I promise not to interfere unless your emotions—pain, fear, doubt, guilt, or suffering—become too overbearing for you to handle. An honest prayer for help is justification enough. I will come to your aid only in those dire moments. To KISS, we can agree to five kinds of prayers with the acronym PHACT: *P* is for praise; *H* is for help; *A* is for adoration; *C* is for contrition; and *T* is for Thanksgiving. Are you okay with this?"

"Yes, that's neat."

"I will be there to assist when you call for help. When you are on your boat, steering your life through eddies and whirlpools, and a big problem occurs, you can call for help in that precise moment in the now. We will be there. I want you to know I will be there to assist only when you call. In addition, the call must be justified! That is Our will.

"When you came into the garden, abused, beaten, battered and on the verge of dying, We heard your call. I came for you in that instance. I wanted you as a child of God." The Man waited, and then said, "Do you accept the challenge? I expect you to answer! Our word is Our bond!" He waited for the boy.

Everything became quiet. It seemed like a breathtaking, blissful eternity sitting under the umbrella of trees with The Man. He knew he had to answer The Man with, "Yes, I accept the challenge." However, yes was a word he couldn't utter.

The Man broke the silence. "I would like you to read about cosmologist Steven Hawking. Would you do that for our next Dialogue?"

Dialogue Twenty-Nine
Steven Hawking[45]

The boy was still acting timid and demure. "Did you read about Steven Hawking?" The Man asked.

The boy pleaded, "Before we talk about Steven Hawking, could you help me with the challenge? I want to accept your challenge, but I don't know enough words to make a bond."

The Man couldn't hold it in. He burst out laughing in joyful response. Through the laughter, he howled, "Oh my gosh, little big man, you can be a hoot and a half. I accept whatever words you have as your bond." He continued in his hilarity.

The boy was completely nonplussed. He had no clue as to what was so funny. "Yeah, I even took notes," he said. "Steven Hawking is a theoretical physicist at the University of Cambridge in the United Kingdom. He is known for his contributions to the fields of theoretical cosmology and quantum gravity, especially in the context of black holes.[46-47]

"His scientific works included theorems regarding singularities in general relativity, and the theoretical discovery that black holes emit radiation, which is known as Hawking radiation. He's written some popular best-selling science books about time and other science ideas."[48]

"What did you think of his ideas?" The Man asked.

"At first, I didn't understand his words from math and physics. After thinking about them, I got the general idea about theorems, general relativity, black holes, and radiation. Physics makes you think." The boy paused before continuing. "He's a brilliant man confined to a wheelchair. His handicap has not slowed his thinking. He's disabled by ALS, known as Lou Gehrig's disease."[49]

The Man interjected, "That gives us a good idea about Steven Hawking. Here are some more of his words. Please read them!" The Man handed the boy some papers.

Before he read the words from Steven Hawking, the boy had to brag: "I think I understand how a scientist can be a prophet of God."

The Man responded with a blank face—no smile or laugh. The

Man's actions bewildered the boy. Not knowing what else to do, he started reading the words from Steven Hawking aloud after a long pause.

Certainly, mathematics has led scientists right to the doorstep of some of the most profound questions of all. First among them is, how did it all begin? In the nature of the physical universe, what could be the explanation for the unreasonable effectiveness of mathematics in explaining nature's behavior?[50]

The boy paused again in his reading. Then he read Steven Hawking's next question: "How can a rational person believe in miracles?" The boy paused again, reflecting on the idea of miracles. Then he read Steven Hawking's answer:

Then we shall all, philosophers, scientists, and just ordinary people, be able to take part in the discussion of the question of why it is that the universe and we exist. For then, we would know the mind of God.[51]

The boy reflected on the words for a moment. Then he continued reading Steven Hawking's words.

Are these mathematical descriptions of reality signposts to some greater intelligence? Is mathematics, along with DNA, another language of God?
[51]

The boy thought that Steven Hawking asked more questions than he did. He persevered in reading from his notes:

In the early nineteen hundreds, most scientists assumed a universe with no beginning and no end. This created certain physical paradoxes, such as how the universe managed to remain stable without collapsing upon itself because of the force of gravity, but other alternatives did not seem attractive.[51]

The boy paused, reflecting again on the words. After a few moments, he started reading again.

The anthropic principle is the idea that our universe is uniquely tuned to give rise to humans. The precise tuning of all of the physical constants and physical laws to make intelligent life possible is not an accident but reflects the action of the one who created the universe in the first place. It would be difficult to explain why the universe should have begun in just this way, except as the act of a God who intended to create beings like us.[51]

Completely overwhelmed by what he read, the boy stopped reading.

The Man said, "Please read Psalms 8 and 19 for next time."

Dialogue Thirty
Learn Many Words and Languages

"Did you read Psalms 8 and 19?" The Man began.

"Yeah, I did! I got my notes right here. I typed my paraphrased words from Psalm 8 first; then I typed what I thought it meant. I understand the Psalm better that way." He read his notes aloud from his laptop. "First in Psalm 8[52]: God's name is majestic. As children of God, we praise Him. Whoever sings of his majesty is using the language of singing as in the Psalms. As soon as you can pronounce it, the divine name enables the believer to share in the glory of His creation. He made us in His image and we are associated with His sovereignty. He will make us strong within ourselves to fulfill our gifts.

"Second: When we look upon his creation, the universe, we will as humans realize how much he cares for us.

"Third: He compares us to the mysterious beings in heaven. He crowns us with glory and beauty. He puts us in charge of all the energies and languages He made. Psalm 8 closes by saying how majestic His name is throughout the universe."

The Man congratulated the boy by saying, "That was a fine summary. How did you come up with that interpretation?"

The boy responded, "Well, first I read it through completely to get an idea of what was being said. Then I went back and read each verse again, using the footnotes. After a while, the words started to make sense. Then I mixed the languages up. Sometimes I used King David's words; sometimes I used the footnote words; sometimes I used your words; and last, sometimes I used my own words. I thought that this is what I am supposed to learn. God wants us to use as many languages as we can learn so we can understand all the laws. Like Solomon, we will reach for the value of wisdom."

The Man was overwhelmed with appreciation for the boy. He liked what He saw. The boy was learning to discipline himself, both in academics and in sports. He was reading at a high level with a good vocabulary. His work ethic and his sports workout routine gave his muscles some definition. He was a nice size for an eighteen-year-old: five feet ten inches tall, around 150 pounds, and a fast sprinter with quick feet. While his high school days would be his highest level of sports, his intellectual and emotional gifts had a long way to go before they reached their limits.

The Man gave the boy a big smile. "Well, little man, instead of being a smart-aleck wise guy, you are becoming a wise man. Do you remember the beatitudes that you hoped you would attain?"

"Yeah!" His eyes moved up and to the right as if he were looking to heaven for the right words. "I have a gift of inner sensitivity. I'm becoming aware when it's working. Ah! I'll always remember the story about Huck kissing the dead. So, I will continue to learn to mourn and feel sadness. I have a moral attitude required for heaven. I am not poor in spirit; I just have a deficiency with words that could keep me from being an educated person. I'll have to work twice as hard.

"I'm becoming conscious of right and wrong. I am gaining in knowledge and understanding and I see Your wisdom. With You, I have counsel. I feel Your kindness, goodness and peace. You are encouraging me to read and write, learn math, science and mostly learn about God."

He paused. "I have a hunger and thirst for righteousness. I must search for something great: like true justice, true good, or true reality. In addition, I must learn to treat others as I would like them to treat me. These will be my 'unto others'." The boy looked over his notes on his computer to see if he had missed anything. He had typed many words into his computer, but he wasn't sure if he understood them. He mumbled until he found the word "emotions" on the screen of his computer. He rattled off his definitions.

"Fear is my own imagination creating prejudices and an impending evil. I feel guilty when I do something wrong. When I don't study or work hard, I have doubts. I am uncertain. Pain can be all kinds of hurts. I hurt myself or I hurt others." He now knew that these feelings, emotions, and words would be his bond. He was just learning to put these emotions into words. He'd laugh and show The Man that he stood behind his words and feelings. His words would be his bond.

He looked up and saw The Man smiling with that mysterious twinkle in his eyes. He was sensitive to The Man's listening to his mumbling. So, rather than feel guilty for not being confident, he put a smile on his own face, and with a twinkle in his eye, he spoke to The Man. "You know, You have shown me nothing but patience. I really do like You. You have been gentle. You do not put me down. Although you have disciplined me a couple of times, you have been extremely kind to me. I do believe that You love me. I feel that I love You too. I'm going to do a lot of 'unto others' for you."

Dialogue Thirty-One
Words, Lyrics, Psalms

"Did you read Psalm 19[53]?" The Man asked the boy.

The boy was sitting cross-legged on the ground, and he replied, "Yes! I also got notes for Psalm 19." He started reading from his notes on his laptop computer.

"First, the universe declares the glory of God. This Psalm celebrates God as the Creator of the universe, particularly the sun and the stars. In the daytime, you see the sun. At night, you see the stars. In the ancient East, the sun symbolized the virtue of justice. Therefore, God, the author of the language for the natural laws and the moral laws manifests His own perfection."

The boy continued with the second point. "I am gaining the knowledge to understand the big bang. When you sang it before, I was too emotional to understand the words. After reading the Psalms, and studying the words, I have a practical sense of the words. For instance, an astronomer, Fred Hoyle,[54] suggested the name big bang, yet there was not a big, loud noise.

"Another for instance: When you sang the words before, they sounded like the choirs of heavenly angels singing them. Now, when I say the same words, they are just practical, boring facts. Listen as I say them. They sure don't have the same lyrics as Yours. Listen!" He recited the words in a monotone.

"The big bang was a silent manifestation into the super force[55]. It came from an infinitesimal volume. The super force expanded at an extraordinary rate, faster than the speed of light for a split second. The super force split into the four main forces that would form the universe: the gravitational, the electromagnetic, and the strong and weak forces of the nucleus. Each force has its own description from mathematical languages. The words are for physicists. They are objective with no emotion.

"See what I mean. These words don't even have the conventional wisdom of street talk." The boy sensed the difference in words for the behavior of each person, startling himself with that leap of thinking.

Each person in the whole world had his or her own words. After a long pause, he came out of his reverie. He reverted to the Psalm.

"Psalm 19 goes on to say that there was no heavenly sound. It is only from the earth and on the earth that God's design stands out. His message reaches the whole earth. However, we have to look with steadfast concentration. We have to work hard to read the message in many different languages.

"Another instance: The Psalms were melodic. The words were pleasing to the ear. The composition and melody gave splendor to the Psalm. My notes go on to say, from the psalmist's time, that this is an allusion to the Assyro-Babylonian idea that the stars are the silent writing of the heavens. I interpreted no speech and silent writings to be the big bang. Its quietness was due to no air or substance to carry a sound.

"Third, the psalmist uses expressions found also in Babylonian mythology. Another example: *High above he pitched a tent for the sun; the sun comes forth like a bridegroom; rises to start the day; delights like a champion; the sun gives off its heat; then sets for the night.*" The boy continued, "For me, this is a metaphor for God doing great things. In these words, you can almost hear the music. I think it is sexual. I hope I can be this romantic when I have sex."

The Man asked, "Do you feel the passion of the Father?"

"Yeah, I do! Even teens know words about sex. I'm being sarcastic—kids talk a lot about sex. The words in the Psalm are more about the passion of love between a man and a woman. I think teenagers are just horny and not passionately in love."

The Man smiled impishly while the boy spoke. The boy picked up The Man's smile and smiled back as he continued.

"Fourth: The natural law of God is perfect, refreshing, trustworthy, and provides wisdom for the simple to the wise. The percepts of God are honest and joyful; the commandment of God is pure. He is the light. These are examples of words praising the language for God's laws.

"You know," the boy said, "a short while ago, I would have had no idea that words used in the Psalms—words you use, and words I am now using—ever existed. When I read the Psalms, I find the words for

God so refreshing and passionate. You know, I think I may be growing up."

The boy looked up at The Man and said, "Verse 9 is about fear. I have trouble with fear! I'm afraid people are going to reject me. I'm still afraid people will hurt me. When we first met, I thought you would hurt me like my dad did. He would whip me, and most of the time, I didn't know why. He would hurt my feelings, especially when he was drinking. I didn't know what to expect. You told me that fear is my own emotion. Then you said to me that my emotional imagination creates prejudices. Different people would reject me; they wouldn't like me; they would hurt me; they'd beat me up."

CHAPTER SIX
An eighteen-year-old boy learns to multitask

Dialogue Thirty-Two
God's Words and Languages Are Sweeter Than Honey

The boy set his laptop down on the ground and stood up. He took a couple of small steps to be closer to The Man. He still had to look up for eye-to-eye contact with The Man, who was standing next to the rock. "You know, I was really self-conscious when I said you were kind and gentle." He paused. "You don't make me feel little. I never believed that anyone would really love me." He paused again. Slowly, and with deep, heartfelt meaning, he said, "I love you."

He waited. The silence was deafening. There was no heavenly sound. The sunlight filtered through the shimmering leaves of the trees. The boy's emotions felt the big bang of quietness. He felt the allusion to the Assyro-Babylonian idea that the sun and stars are the silent writing of the heavens. The sun symbolized the virtue of justice. He knew he had to work hard to find the message of this beatitude: *Justice came with forgiving and loving.* He truly believed the feelings he had within himself, so different from abuse.

The boy was a little embarrassed by his open confession of love. He was fidgety. Breaking the silence was like a bolt of lightning and a clap of thunder happening simultaneously. He whispered, "You explained the three *omnis* and one *bene* so I would understand that I need the feelings of fear, pain, and guilt, but not the prejudice to a great extent. Is this a child of God?"

The Man didn't respond.

The boy turned to pick up his computer. Trying to cover his nervousness, his voice squeaked as he said, "From Psalm 19, my notes say this." He cleared his throat. "The Fifth point: The fear of being separated from God is pure, lasting forever; the judgments of God are true, upright, every one more desirable than gold; His words are sweeter than honey. Our emotions of fear and guilt are needed to love God.

"From verses 10 and 11, I understood that God's words and languages are sweeter than honey," the boy admitted. "No matter what book or version of the Bible I read; no matter what word I say or hear, the words themselves are sweeter than honey. Because I now understand that words bring forth feelings and emotions. They are associated with virtues or cardinal virtues. I now understand that words also bring forth feelings and emotions associated with vices or cardinal vices. Words describe goodness, and words describe evil."

He looked for approval from The Man. The Man nodded and gestured for more with His hands. "Words are like the toy boat," the boy continued. "The boat's path is detoured by an eddy or whirlpool and takes on a new path. The same exact words spoken by different speakers take on different meanings. The speaker's stance, inflection, gestures, loudness, pitch, rhythm, syntax, and tone all affect his meaning. I am finding the same problems with the written word. "Words are a treasure hunt for the reader. Words, behavior, feelings, and emotions cannot be separated."

The Man grinned at the boy's excitement.

"I'm learning so much about words. For instance, moral or chaste behavior is an outward sign of a feeling or emotion associated with a virtuous word. For example, in my Bible, there are reference notes in the margins and footnotes below. Psalm 19 referred me to Romans 1:18[56] 'The retribution of God from heaven is being revealed against the ungodliness and injustice of human beings who in their injustice hold back the truth.'

"My treasure hunt for words translated this to mean: God directs His emotion of anger—usually a cardinal sin, but in this case *just* anger—at the evil, emotional, biased behavior of men who hinder the truth ... a virtue. God uses an emotional vice to overcome an emotional vice and save a virtue." The boy looked over at The Man. "Is this interpretation of virtues and vices okay?"

The Man nodded and said, "It will do."

"All right! I have another reference that I put in my notes: Immoral or evil behavior is the outward sign of a feeling or emotion associated with an act of a vice. For example: Psalm 19 referred me to Romans 2:1[57] So no matter who you are, if you pass judgment, you have no excuse. It is yourself that you condemn when you judge others, since you believe in the same way as those you are condemning. In the new words that I am learning, I translated this to mean that to pretend to use a cardinal virtue, or judgment, is a hypocritical, emotional behavior when you do not possess the prudence of the virtue. You convict yourself by your hypocritical, contradictory behavior. God's judgment is just when dealing with this kind of behavior.

"I'm learning to use some big words. I actually understand the words," the boy confessed.

The Man interrupted. "You did well! Now, how do you like using highfalutin words?"

They laughed, the boy just as uproariously as The Man.

Dialogue Thirty-Three
The Garden, Security Haven

They were in the garden, under the shade of the trees. This was the boy's sanctuary, his secret haven. Here he could talk to The Man. He started telling The Man about the latest thoughts he had typed into his laptop computer, even though they were somewhat unconnected.

"I do understand that God's words and languages are sweeter than honey. I worked hard to understand feelings and emotions, virtues and vices, and how they relate to words. I don't feel fear, pain, doubt, or guilt as much anymore. What I mean is that I feel my emotions, but I'm not afraid of them. I think my fear of God is a sense that if I don't live up to what He has given me, then I won't realize His love for me.

"I must rely on God's words and languages being sweeter than honey. I must struggle and work as hard as I can to learn as much as I can. When I'm having an emotional attack, You said to call! You promised that You would teach me to walk in Your light. I'm beginning to think this is the concept of the three *omni* and one *bene* words."

The Man slapped his thighs and roared with laughter. "You make me laugh! You get so serious when you discover something new. You want people to think you are so smart. The Father's words are sweeter than honey. So just remember that you catch more flies with honey than you do with vinegar."

The Man kept teasing the boy. "Okay, mister little big man, lighten up! Use levity! Humor, puns, sarcasm, irony, and double and triple entrendes will lighten up anyone's day. Make use of humor sprinkled on your words. The old harsh, hurtful trash talk was not really your best style.

"I want you to read Paul's[58] Letters to the Romans and Galatians[59]. Compare your style with Paul's. He was a lawyer, and you can never be Paul. However, you can cherish his words as a prophet. Type the keywords 'Saint Paul, the Apostle' into your computer. Summarize what you see."

The boy harshly interrupted. "But I haven't finished Psalm 19."

Serenely, The Man spoke. "That's okay! We will come back to it later." The Man then cracked up with a hearty laugh as He said, "You are learning to multitask. That is a fine skill to possess."

The boy did as The Man suggested. He summarized into his computer. The Man waited patiently as the boy took his time with the assignment. After a long while, the boy finished reading and typing. He raised his head.

The boy beamed with pride. He said. "Am I getting across the main ideas when I summarize with short sentences?"

The Man was having a ball teaching the boy. "Yes, they are fine! We'll make a theatrical play of the Letters to the Romans and Galatians later."

"Wow! That Paul is some kind of awesome writer. His sentences are long and hard to read, though. I was even reading the easiest translation. I don't know if I could act in a play using an older version with old-time words."

The boy read aloud what he typed: "The Epistle of Paul to the Romans is loaded with serious language and the words of a lawyer. The Epistle of Paul to the Galatians is full of words that explain and teach the moral laws. The words in the Epistles are probably translations from Hebrew, to Greek, to Latin, to two or more translations into English.

He stopped reading. "I'll stick with math. It's easier for me. How many languages do you know?" he asked The Man.

"I helped put all of them in the medium!" The Man responded.

The boy couldn't believe his ears. He continued trying to impress The Man with his newly learned words.

He spoke aloud as he typed. "My fear is that I won't work hard enough to learn all the words of Paul—omnipresent. I don't know if I have the capability to learn all his words —omniscient. I don't know if I can overcome my own prejudices and biases—omnipotent. I don't know if I can please You and the Father—beneficence." He turned to look at The Man.

"Boy! Look at all the doubts I have." He sat down on his haunches, trying to bring to mind what he would do when he felt fearful or guilty. He sensed it had to do with the concept of power and his intellect. Not finding any quick solutions, he read aloud his notes on his computer about Psalm 19.

"Psalms 19:11–14[60] starts by saying that I will be formed by God's words. If I learn the words and laws, I will obtain great rewards. However, who can detect his own failings? Who will cleanse me of my unknown faults? Who will preserve me from pride and never let it be my master? Who will make me above reproach and free from grave sin? May the words of my mind, heart, and soul always find favor in the Father's presence and in You. You are my rock and redeemer."

The solution was right here in the Psalm. He started typing:

I don't know The Man's name! Oh well, I'll just call him The Man. This is first thing I have to do—show Him respect and love. I have to start thinking positive thoughts. I have to get rid of doubt and be aware of it when I feel it. Be positive! Get fired up! I will learn the proper use of power rather than forcing my power on others. I'll handle fear and guilt when they come up. My intellect is where I have to get to work. Learn, baby, learn.

Dialogue Thirty-Four
The Dream, Scaling Mountains

The solutions were now in his notes. He was learning to put more information on his hard drive. The Man was the key to understanding all the information and knowledge on his hard drive. He said to The Man, "I have these worries. Will you help me?"

The Man was quiet. The boy had just read aloud what was on the computer. "If I fail to recognize the painful feeling of impending danger, then will you teach me to listen to God's words about the emotions associated with fear?"

He looked at The Man, pleading for help. "Yes!" said The Man.

"If I fail to recognize the conscious violation of a law; then will you teach me to listen to God's words about the emotions associated with guilt?" Again, he pleaded.

The Man nodded, touched his heart with his right fist, and said, "Yes!"

"If I fail to recognize the certainty of a truth or fail to recognize the ambiguous uncertainty of an opinion, then will you teach me to listen to God's words about the emotions associated with doubt?"

"Yes!" The Man said emphatically. "I can wash away your hidden faults, pride, anger, and greed." The Man stared intently at the boy. The boy gazed awkwardly at The Man. They were eye-to-eye. He had an answer in his heart. He voiced what he was feeling.

"I can't get rid of my hidden faults! I must call for The Man from my boat."

"You got that right!" The Man answered. The Man was about to say more, when the boy interrupted.

"Oh!" he barked. I have to tell you about the other night." Energized, the boy just had to tell The Man what had taken place. He looked down at his notes. "You would never believe what has happened to me! I had finished typing my notes into my laptop. I was rereading Psalm 19 when a slight breeze blew the pages of my Bible. It flew open to Psalm 27.[61] The words jumped off the page and into my heart. 'In God's company there is no fear.'

"I started reading and writing because I wanted to share with you my words of translation." His excitement brought on a new trait of slight stuttering as he read his Psalm 27 notes. "You, my b-b-big Man, are my light and my d-deliverance from all the evil and b-b-b-bad things. I know now that my greatest fear is that I will not live up t-to Your words You have about me."

The Man caringly put his arm around the boy's shoulder. With the other hand, palm down, The Man motioned for the boy to slow down.

The boy took a deep breath. "I now know that when people try to hurt me, my heart, soul, and mind will not fear. I must learn as Peter learned: 'My trust in you will never be shaken.'" He was now at ease.

"The one thing I seek to enjoy is the sweetness of being with You, as we are in these Dialogues. I will make music for my Man. I will sing. I will learn words. I will learn the languages of God. First, verse 10[62] in Psalm 27 is about my father and mother forsaking me. That is no longer a big deal. I don't feel the pain of rejection or abandonment from them any more. I don't feel any fear of abuse.

"The rest of the verses in Psalm 27 are about how You are going to teach me to see the goodness in God. By putting my hope in You, my b-big Man, I will be strong and b-bold in my heart, mind, and soul. I can be a child of God." He again took a deep gulp of air. He calmed down.

"Before I went to bed, and before I went to sleep, I had thoughts of what I would like to be when I go to college. I like math. I am also good at it. However, science tickles me. Biology, chemistry, physiology, physics, and other science subjects are all exciting to learn. Well, I fell asleep before I could decide." He paused to take a breath. He made eye contact with The Man. They both broke out with huge smiles.

"That same night, after studying Psalm 27 and thinking about math and science, I had a dream of solving physics problems. I dreamed I could be a physicist. Then, in the dream, came a story about a scientist[63] who had lived by his faith in the power of reason. I dreamed I tried to be like that, but my power of reason was dumber than a jackass who misuses his power. Well, the scientist's story almost ended like a bad nightmare for him. My story got all jumbled up, leading nowhere. I dreamed we were both scaling the mountains of ignorance: he was about to conquer the highest peak; I was way down on another mountain, still trying to follow him.

"As he pulled himself over the final rock at the top, he yelled praises to God. In my dream, I hurried as fast as I could to see what he found. He was with a band of angels who had been sitting there for centuries, discussing theology. They greeted me as an achiever. The dream ended before I could find what I had achieved."

Dialogue Thirty-Five
Notes in the Computer

"I knew after reading Psalm 27, and remembering the dream, that my faith, hope, and love had to be for You, my big Man. Your bad nightmare was the Crucifixion. The scaling of the mountain was Your Resurrection. If I follow, You would help me scale mountains, both in science and in theology." The boy and The Man smiled.

The boy then referred back to his notes. "Calling for help is humbling. With humility, You, my Man, will never let pride be my master." His notes included thoughts he must remember. "With God's help, I will be free from grave sin. Call from the boat! I can't be afraid to call for help." He felt an awkward moment. He mumbled other notes. "May my languages always find favor? I must learn to listen with my heart, mind, and soul as a child of God. God is my rock, my redeemer." He stopped reading the notes from his laptop.

The Man rose from the rock. "Let's walk." He stretched and reached down for the boy's hand. They started walking, leaving the large boulder. Their walk quickly took them from the tree-shaded garden, where light flickered filtered through. They walked into the bright sunshine.

The Man started, "So you think I can help you scale the mountains of science and theology?" Without waiting for an answer, The Man asked another question: "Do you remember that just before you read the words from Steven Hawking, you had to brag with the following words: 'I think I understand how a scientist can be a prophet of God'?

"Yeah, I remember!" said the boy. "Was it wrong of me to brag? Was I showing the sin of pride?"

The Man responded. "How did you feel? How did you say the words?"

The boy withdrew into himself. He tried to remember how he felt. He still held The Man's hand. It felt warm and good. He felt secure. After a few moments of reflection, he replied, "I felt as if I knew the answer for the prophets. I wanted to share with You the answer so You would be proud of me for being smart. I probably said the words like a smart aleck. However, more than anything, I wanted to please You. I wanted to tell You about prophets."

"That is good!" He said. "I do think you understand on two levels, whether you realize it or not. First, you know that pride is a sin. Arrogance, haughtiness, conceit, and narcissism are a few behaviors of sin, like pride. Second, you know that pride is not a sin if accompanied by being lawful, wise, knowledgeable, righteous, tactful, tolerant, or loving. You worked hard to increase your knowledge!"

"Yeah, I did! I say this because it is the truth. But I don't think it is the tactful thing to say."

The Man paused to let his words sink in. To start up the conversation again, He said, "What did you do to bring about this understanding?"

The boy replied, "I went to that part of the Bible that explained about prophets. I studied the Bible's words. I read history books. I watched TV stories about different prophets. I watched movies. I took notes! I tried to find out if a particular scientist believed in God. I had a concern about what religion a scientist believed was his."

"The sun was still shining bright in the afternoon. They still held hands. The Man felt this was a teachable moment.

The boy felt no shame holding hands with The Man. There was no doubt in his mind that there was nothing wrong with an eighteen-year-old boy holding The Man's hand. The solution was right here in this lesson. He began to type:

We have shown each other respect and love on a high level. It is only for others to judge us with their misuse of power by regulating us with a culture of rules that abuses us. We surely have not abused each other. Be positive! Get fired up! Learn, baby, learn. Multitask.

My intellect learned how a scientist could be a prophet of God—how science and theology could be compatible. My heart and soul learned about feelings, power, rules and regulations, and a new word that fits its cultural mores.

The boy stopped typing and returned his attention to The Man. "The first thing my notes state about Prophets is this: The great religions always had their 'inspired' speakers. Men and women who claimed to pronounce in the name of God were prophets. They were aware that their message came from God. They were the bearers and interpreters of the Word of God. Their mission was to the people of their own time. Their message relates to both present and future. To the people they communicated the language of God."

Dialogue Thirty-Six
The Age of the Earth, According to Scientists

The boy continued to read his notes from his laptop. He was beginning to understand that his computer, hooked up to the Internet, was similar to the medium where God stored all his information and knowledge. It wasn't difficult to understand once you had some ideas of the concepts of system theory. He was pleased with himself as he retrieved the knowledge of the prophets. He liked writing short sentences rather than the long ones St. Paul used. He read aloud to make sure of the main concept.

"The father of all prophets was Moses. He scaled Mount Sinai. He spoke with God face-to-face. Moses conveyed the moral laws to the chosen people. His words came directly from God." The boy was getting a little excited. "I found out that prophets used words and language to praise God. Sharing languages with others is good. To honor God as the true author is good. It is indeed a prophet of God who does this."

"Well, my little big man, it seems you have again done your homework," The Man responded proudly. "Here are some words from Steven Hawking, Ilya Prigogine, and Francis Collins. You do remember that they are brilliant scientists. Please read their words aloud. We shall see if they are prophets," He persisted. The boy felt important reading aloud to The Man.

"Yeah! I remember them." He read their words:

There is additional compelling evidence for the correctness of the big bang. Background noise was coming from the universe itself. That was the kind of afterglow expected because of the big bang. Physicists agree that the universe began as an infinitely dense, dimensionless point of pure energy. The existence of the big bang begs the question of what came before that. In addition, who was responsible?[64]

The boy uttered aloud his own thoughts, adding to those of the scientists: "The natural laws must be in harmony with the moral laws."

"Well," The Man said, "do you think Steven Hawking, for an example, fills the role of a prophet?"

"I dunno! He's pretty close. I'll have to study my notes to see if he fits," the boy said, not knowing how or what to answer.

"Okay," The Man said. "Let us read more of their words. Studying their words and your notes should give us a good idea of how to find the role of a prophet for scientists, if any."

The boy rose in a dramatic flamboyance from his yoga position to portray a standing, poised prophet. He performed a pirouette with ease as he kept his laptop open and balanced the scientists' pages of words on top of his computer. Reading aloud in the deepest resonance of voice he could muster, he tried to orate as Steven Hawking would through his voice box.

Scientists believe our sun did not form in the early days of the universe.[65] *Our sun is probably a second or third generation star. A local recoalescence formed the sun about five billion years ago. As that was occurring, a small proportion of heavier elements in the vicinity escaped incorporation into the new star. Instead, they collected into the planets that now rotate around our sun.*[66]

Strongly invigorated, he stopped reading and, reverting to his former attitude of acting out as an abused kid who was now the adult abuser, challenged, "Hey, wait a minute! I can add and subtract. Fourteen billion minus five billion equals nine billion. Do scientists believe that the universe just existed for nine billion years before our sun came into existence? I don't know if I can buy that!"

He hesitated. Sarcastically, he said, "Let's see if these scientists have any more baloney." He started reading their words again, rapidly, in his own voice, without inflections.

This includes our own planet. The earth was far from hospitable in its early days. Initially it was very hot. Continual massive collisions bombarded the earth. It gradually cooled and developed an atmosphere. Then it became potentially hospitable to living things by about four billion years ago. A mere hundred and fifty million years later, the earth was teeming with life.[67]

The boy was astounded! "Wow! That's a long time. From what I know, humans like us have only been on the earth about eighty to ninety thousand years."

Dialogue Thirty-Seven
Prophets-Scientists Test

The Man sat with His back against the tree. His hands relaxed, resting on His bent knees. The boy stood in silence, looking at The Man for some guidance. Getting none, he returned to read the accumulated words of many scientists. He tried to read the words on his computer screen as he thought Francis Collins or Steven Hawking would. He liked imitating his idols as he read the words aloud.

Only second or third generation stars and their accompanying planetary systems would carry the potential of the heavier elements. These types of stars came into existence five to ten billion years after the big bang. Carbon and oxygen are the heavy elements necessary for life. Even then, a great deal of time would be necessary for life to reach sentience and intelligence.[68]

Again, the boy looked for guidance and reassurance. "Well," The Man asked, "do you *now* think Steven Hawking, as our example, fills the role of a prophet?"

The boy hated answering questions for which he didn't have a clue. Being cute, he tried reversing by asking, "Can we make a test for a prophet?"

"Sure," The Man responded. "Show me the test." The Man enjoyed playing this little game with the boy, watching him paint himself into a corner.

The boy began whispering to himself. "Okay, let's see. How about a scoring system? I think I got it; a score of ten is excellent. A score of five is okay. A one is bad.

"Okay," the boy said to The Man, "let's see if Steven Hawking is a prophet-scientist. If science is like a religion, then Hawking would get a ten on 'religions always had their inspired speakers.' He would get a four on 'to pronounce in the name of God.' He would get a six on being aware that 'his message came from God.' He would get a ten on being 'the bearer and interpreter of the mathematical Word of God.' He would get eights on 'the mission to the people of his own time,' for 'being a prophet like Moses.' And for his 'message to both present and future,' he would get a ten for 'communicating the mathematical language of God.' He would get a five for 'using words and language to praise God.' He would get a three for 'sharing a language that God was the true author.'"

"This is a dumb test. It's simpleminded. The only thing good about it are some numbers," challenged The Man. The Man spoke thoughtfully to the disappointed boy. "Having numbers, is that what you think of your test? Do you think we can get some idea of whether a scientist is a prophet?" The Man continued to play the game, gently urging the boy to raise the bar of excellence.

"I think," said the boy timidly, "that the test is too simple and dumb. Steven Hawking got a score of seventy-two out of one hundred. A score of seventy-two would probably be the average for most scientists. He was doing what most scientists would do, although he may be the leader in his field." Timid with his words and hesitant in his voice, the boy tried a new slant.

"I think that scientists believe in the language of mathematics. They believe in their statistics and probabilities. They believe in their empirical theories. The seventy-two is a weak statistic that agrees with a weak yes on the *maybe* side, which has no mathematical relevance at all. Mathematics describes theories based on experiments. God is personal. It's just a guess of whether scientists believe in God. The same guess would probably say they do not believe in any one religion."

The Man smiled slightly. He didn't want to outright laugh at the boy. He was just letting the boy work things out for himself. When he couldn't climb out of his hole, The Man would reach down and help him with his ideas, but only after the boy called for help.

The boy stubbornly continued to consider whether scientists were prophets. "They might believe in a deist like Einstein did. Scientists also like to use big words and long sentences. I tried to simplify their writings and their words, but in the end, it was easier to learn and understand their language. KISS: Keep it simple, scientist."

The boy was struggling, trying hard to get back on track with his explanation. He reverted to the scientist's explanations. "I've taken some notes from other scientists I'd like to share with You—and hear what You think. I got these ideas from watching a few DVDs, watching

TV, and, of course, reading books. These ideas were the conclusions of many scientists."

Dialogue Thirty-Eight
Origin of the Universe

The boy sat in frustration with his back against a tree, his legs bent slightly at the knees but otherwise stretched out. His computer sat on his thighs. He was concentrating on the dim screen. The sunlight under the tree was fading as the shade increased in the late afternoon. "Scientists generally agree that the origin of the universe is increasingly well understood," he read aloud. "So, too, is our own sun and solar system. Scientists consider the following three observations." He read aloud:

Number one:[69] *The creation of matter and antimatter came about in almost equivalent amounts in the early moments following the big bang. At one millisecond of time, the universe cooled. Matter and antimatter condensed. They encountered each other. Complete annihilation was the result. Each contact released a photon of energy.*

The boy thought, *This was the same idea as before, but just slightly different words.* He continued to read aloud:

The symmetry between matter and antimatter was not precise. It is in that tiny fraction of a second that the initial potentiality of the universe came about. Created, as we now know it, was the mass of the entire universe.

The boy was on a roll. It pepped him up. He recognized the smile on The Man as he spoke to Him.

If there had been complete symmetry between matter and antimatter, the universe would quickly have devolved into pure radiation. People, planets, stars, and galaxies would never have come into existence.

The Man gestured with His hands on His knees to give Him more.

Excitedly the boy said, "Number two:[70] The way in which the universe expanded after the big bang depended critically on how much total mass and energy it had." *This clarifies the concept a little,* he thought. He continued reading aloud:

The strength of the gravitational constant was crucial. The incredible degree of fine-tuning of all the physical constants has been a subject of wonder for many experts. It is still astonishing.

Why did the universe start out with so nearly the critical rate of expansion? It is still expanding at nearly the same critical rate. It would have recollapsed, if smaller than one part in one hundred thousand million million. On the other hand, if the rate of expansion had been greater by even one part in a million, stars and planets could not have been able to form.

The boy was amazed by this awesome concept. Not only was the mathematics awesome, but there was also an awesome artistic beauty about it. My emotions and intellect are in harmony. I think of God as being a loving mathematician. Words, intellect, emotions, and feelings exist together as one. He enthusiastically told The Man, "The existence of the universe as we know it rests upon a knife edge of improbability."

The boy asked The Man, "Could the observations in numbers one and two be miracles?"

The Man didn't answer aloud. He just gestured for the boy to give Him more.

The boy continued to read from his notes on the computer screen.

Number three.[71] The same remarkable circumstance applies to the formation of heavier elements. If the strong nuclear force had been slightly weaker, then only hydrogen could have formed in the universe. A slightly stronger "strong nuclear force" would convert all the hydrogen into helium. Instead, only twenty-five percent of all helium occurred early in the big bang.

"Man! This astrophysics stuff is something!" He was so excited to be learning so much about space, the arrow of time, galaxies, solar systems, stars, planets, and so on. He read:

This ability to generate the heavier elements depended upon the fusion furnaces of stars. Otherwise, the heavy elements could not be born.

The boy was so excited that he continued without taking a breath. "Can you believe that? The stars are like furnaces! Adding to this remarkable observation, tuning the nuclear force just sufficiently for carbon to form is the critical aspect for life forms on Earth. Converting all the carbon into oxygen would occur with a slightly more attractive force.[72]

"Oh my God!" the boy cried out.

The Man shook his head slowly and bowed it in reverence to His Father. He could easily forgive the boy for his action, but not for the words of disrespect.

Dialogue Thirty-Nine
Redeemed Scientists and Prophets

The boy looked over at The Man. He felt somewhat secure, but in the back of his mind, he was puzzled. He liked puzzles. He liked asking questions to solve his puzzles.

"I'm finished for the moment with these ideas from scientists," he said. "I understand their three observations. Their explanations are satisfying and exciting when you stay within the awareness of what they know as scientists. Each of their theories has laws and a set of rules. I have much more information in my notes about scientists that I still need to process.

"You know, I don't think I can make a case for scientists being prophets of God. In the Bible, the job was to be a prophet. Even so," the boy went on, "I think I redeemed myself. Our Dialogues could be like two people having a conversation. We shared our conversation with others, just like prophets. Yeah! With Your help, I could be a prophet. Let's see what happens if I rewrite the ten things about prophets."[73]

The boy was inspired to share his newfound knowledge. He rewrote each thing about the prophets with enthusiasm:

1. We could be like inspired speakers.
2. We would be pronouncing in the name of the Father, Son. and Holy Spirit.
3. We would hope that this message came from God.
4. We are the bearers and interpreters of the mathematical languages used in the Dialogues.
5. We accepted the mission to the people of our time.
6. Moses brought the moral laws; we would bring the natural laws.
7. We would hope our message gets to the present and future people.
8. We shared languages with our Bible study groups.
9. We have used words and language to praise God.
10. We have honored God as the true author of all languages.

"Yeah! I feel our Dialogues prove the point about prophets and scientists."

The boy looked up at The Man as He arose from His sitting position against the tree. The Man stood now with His hands on His hips. His eyebrows raised as the twinkle in His eyes gave way to a colossal smile that became a thunderous laugh. The laughter was contagious, and the boy joined in. He set his computer down and closed the screen. He jumped up, agile as a cat.

The Man and the boy exchanged high fives and low fives. The boy did a little Indian victory dance. To go along with his high-stepping knee kicks and stomping feet, he whooped and hollered for ten or fifteen minutes.

The Man was laughing uproariously. He was cheering the boy onward, clapping His hands.

The boy stopped suddenly, unable to believe the thoughts that had come to him. The boy repeated Steven Hawking's question and answer from before, with a change from "how" and "then" to *when*.

How *When* may a rational person believe in miracles?

Then *When* we shall all, philosophers, scientists, and just ordinary people, take part in the discussion of the question of why it is that the universe and we exist. For then we would know the mind of God. We are His miracles.

The Man also referred to Steven Hawking. As Steven Hawking points out, humans could still imagine a set of laws that determines events completely. A supernatural being could observe, using these laws, the present state of the universe, without disturbing it.

CHAPTER SEVEN
An eighteen-year-old boy learns to compare

Dialogue Forty
Emulate The Man

The Man restated Steven Hawking. Humans could still imagine a set of laws that determine events completely. Using these laws, a supernatural being could observe the present state of the universe without disturbing it.

"The medium is available for seeking the language of these laws," The Man said authoritatively.

The boy was wordless! He started thinking. Then his thoughts turned to words describing the pictures he saw in his mind's eye. He wanted help from The Man. "Let me see if I have this right. You said that all languages are stored in the medium, which is available for humans to learn languages and mathematics. We will reach the stage where our moral, natural, and scientific laws are consistent and in harmony with our own evolution. Is that right?"

Barely visible, The Man nodded His head.

The boy was frustrated. There was no order to his thinking. It was a bunch of gibberish questions and answers. He was bewildered and wanted more help from The Man. Even his *Get fired up!* and *Learn, baby, learn* were not kicking in with any help.

The Man understood and was quiet.

The boy spoke loudly to The Man. "A new language for a new set of laws is still unknown. Languages are hard enough to learn. All the different sciences use different words now. Everybody creates his or her own big words and long sentences. It is as if the groups of people want to create their own Tower of Babel. In their tower only one language will be spoken." The boy kept on babbling. "However, a new set of laws depends on the constants. Current theory cannot predict the values of the fifteen physical constants. They are givens—they simply have the value that they have."

Stopping to reflect, the boy realized he was babbling. He was like the people who had the diversity of languages introduced on Earth at the Tower of Babel. As he continued to spout off his newfound words and knowledge, he became conscious of the syntax. He tried to put his thoughts into some rational order. He took a deep breath. He tried to relax his mind and body. He spoke slowly.

"The chance that all of these constants would take on the values necessary to result in a stable universe capable of sustaining complex life forms was almost infinitesimal." He looked up at The Man. "Do we realize this tiny number? This is a tiny number; even Blaise Pascal[74] wouldn't hedge his bet on these odds.

"My mind is getting cluttered. According to science, we shouldn't be here. Our universe is wildly improbable." The maturing eighteen-year-old boy was actually bewildered. Yet in opposition, he was cool, calm, and collected. He had faith in The Man. His heart and soul were at peace. He was gaining the Wisdom of Solomon.

He believed humans could find the proper languages, just as they found other languages after the Tower of Babel. The boy knew he had to study the ideas from different scientists. He had to know their history to reduce the clutter in his head. Math and science could at least clarify complex concepts. More important, though, was the desire and ability to emulate the faith, gentleness, and goodness of The Man. Acquiring His humility, joy, and patience was the goal.

He crammed studies, ideas, and experiments from different scientists and eras into his laptop computer. He again thought his computer with its hard drive resembled God's medium. He was learning to store information and knowledge in his laptop. However, he still had to understand what he was putting into the laptop. It was like Humpty Dumpty. His information could be scattered to smithereens. Then again, like the toy boat, he couldn't predict where the information was going to be. He had to learn ways to organize.

The Man led him to the right processes. The Man helped him gain self-control. Once he was somewhat organized, he liked to share his new knowledge with The Man. The Man always helped to clarify his ideas, thereby increasing his understanding. He knew The Man talked to his whole being as a child of God, no matter what actual age he was.

Dialogue Forty-One
The Man Accomplished His Strategy

They were sitting in their usual place under the shade of the trees. The boy had amassed a storehouse of information about math and science. "Would you comment on my interpretations?" he asked The Man. They laughed because they'd both had the same idea simultaneously.

The boy spoke. "Were you thinking I was on my boat and calling for help?" They bumped knuckles on their closed right fists.

The Man nodded his head, and whispered, "No problem. When you ask, I will be there."

They laughed some more.

It was always a thrill for the boy to read aloud to The Man. He read aloud from his notes to hear how The Man would respond. "The French astronomer and mathematician Pierre Simon La Place,[75] of the early 1800s, said that once the initial configuration of the universe was established, all other future events, including those involving human experiences of the past, present, and future were irreversibly specified. This is an extreme form of scientific determinism, leaving no place for God except at the beginning. The toy boats would have exact predictable paths, according to LaPlace," the boy added.

"You now know that this cannot be true!" The Man responded. "But it's not bad for a beginning."

It was great having his laptop with all this data. The Boy read his next entry aloud. "In the early 1900s, quantum mechanics[76] overturned precise scientific determinism. Planck and Einstein demonstrated that light did not come in all possible energies, but was quantized in particles of precise energy, known as photons. Heisenberg's uncertainty principle[77] is where the energy multiplied by the time of a small particle can never be accurately determined simultaneously. One might be able to determine the energy, but time will then be widely unknown. The same happens with momentum multiplied by distance. You can determine the position in space, but the momentum of a particle will be unknown. For example, on a much larger scale, you could determine the momentum and direction of the toy boat, but not know exactly where it is. Or, if you know where it is, then you wouldn't know its momentum and direction."

"You are getting good at your simple explanations." The Man gave him a slap on the back. The boy coughed and leaped forward with his right foot to keep his equilibrium. He balanced his laptop. He showed the screen to The Man.

"This next scientist is best seen on the screen of the computer. The equation is easier to see in a simple way on the screen. Scientist Frank Drake[78] was a radio astronomer in 1961. With his famous equation, he considered what the probabilities might be for life to exist elsewhere in the universe. The number of communicating civilizations—or cc—in our own galaxy might be the product of seven factors." He held up the laptop to show the equation of factors:

[79](cc) = 1st x 2nd x 3rd x 4th x 5th x 6th x 7th

First Factor: The number of stars in the Milky Way (about 100 billion), times

Second Factor: Fraction of stars with planets, times

Third Factor: Number of planets capable of sustaining life, times

Fourth Factor: Fraction of planets where life evolves, times

Fifth Factor: Fraction where the evolving life is intelligent, times

Sixth Factor: Fraction that developed the ability to communicate, times

Seventh Factor: Fraction of planets' life during which the ability to communicate overlaps with ours. The earth is approximately 4.5 billion years old, so the last factor reflects only a tiny fraction—0.000000022—of the earth's existence.

The boy then said, "Frank Drake said that there is a small chance that life forms can exist elsewhere in the universe."

The Man was impressed with the information that the boy had accumulated. However, He directed the boy to a more meaningful discussion, doing so without hurting the boy's feelings. He stopped the boy with a question: "Do you remember our discussion about Nobel

Prize—winning chemist Ilya Prigogine? Do you have his ideas on your computer?"

After a minute of searching, the boy replied, "Yeah, here he is! He wrote a book called *The End of Certainty*. Do you want me to read my notes?"

The Man had accomplished His strategy. "If you would not mind," he said.

In the back of his mind, the boy knew The Man had tricked him. The Man was so obvious. He smiled to himself. The honesty of The Man was apparent even during a con.

Dialogue Forty-Two
An Egghead from Harvard

The Man smiled at the boy. He had not tricked him. He knew the boy's favorite movie was *The Sting*, with Robert Redford and Paul Newman as con men who preyed on people. The people were called tricks. To turn a trick was to cheat a person. The Man and the boy liked the same things. This was an honest, obvious sting between The Man and the boy. It was a win-win. He led the boy. The boy followed.

They looked at each other. Each took his forefinger and flicked his nose. Redford and Newman had used the same signal. This was an understanding that they had the trick in the palm of their hands with a flick of their nose. Their laughter was so real. Still laughing, the boy went back to work. His work ethic was getting better.

He read aloud what Professor Prigogine had asserted:

Classical science[80] emphasized order and stability; now in contrast, we see in modern science fluctuations, instability, multiple choices, and limited predictability at all levels of observation. All of science includes instability and chaos. We then obtain a formulation of the laws of nature appropriate for the description of our evolving universe, a description that contains the arrow of time.

"All the laws of science have limitations in their particular system of endeavor," The Man added. "There is no trick or sting. Each science had its own set of laws, its own set of rules, and its own limitations. "Do you understand the professor's words and ideas, and what I added? Do you think scientists try to trick people with their theories?"

"No!" said the boy. "It's not a trick. I think I understand! If I use my toy boat as a metaphor, I can change the professor's words to my words." He mimicked the professor: "'I assert: Classical science says you can predict the path, the place, and the speed of the toy boat. The new science uses probabilities and the math of chaos theory. It says you can't predict the exact path, the place, or the speed of the boat.'

"My words assert. The arrow of time is like the water in the creek. We humans go with the flow of the arrow of time. The water flows in one direction, but has eddies and whirlpools in it that interferes with the boat's place, speed and direction. If you skim with an eddy, you go faster. If you drift against an eddy, you go slower. Sometimes we humans seem to go fast in time and sometimes we seem to go slow. We must look for the appropriate language that describes our changes and learn to adapt to them."

"Oh, my little big man. You are getting there, in the now. You are learning to use your intuition and logic simultaneously. You will surely enhance your intellect. You will surely enhance your feelings and emotions. You will overcome the negative aspects of abuse. You are ready to go to college. Read some more of the professor's ideas."

"Thank you for the compliment," said the boy shyly. His face was a little pink with embarrassment as he continued to read: "The professor said that past and future no longer play symmetrical roles. Once instability is included, we can no longer predict the future with certainty, or retrodict the past.[81] Science is a dialogue between humankind and nature. A time-reversible world would be an unknowable world, making a dialogue impossible. Interaction between the knower and the known creates a difference between past and future."[82]

"Stop there," said The Man. "What happens to your boat, in your words?"

The boy took a deep breath. He'd been thinking about time for the last year or so, ever since the watchmaker and his physics classes. "Well, let's see. If you look behind the boat to see where you've been, and what you know, you're okay. You can talk about the past because you know it. However, you can't turn the boat around and go into the past and talk about it, change it, or repeat it.

"While you are talking about the past, you are not in the now, so you miss some of the present. When you turn to look ahead into the future, you have to steer and work hard to get around or through the eddies and whirlpools. You're interacting with nature in the present. You have new problems to solve. You are involved in your environment and in your cultures. You know what you know.

"You are passing new tests, trials, and tribulations. If you change the state of the boat by a tiny amount, you change its future significantly. The future is different from the past. There are new rivers to explore, whether you like it or not. So past and future are not symmetrical. The past is not equal to the future.

"Once instability, a test, trial, or tribulation is included, you can't predict the future with any certainty. In addition, you can't recreate the past with certainty because you've missed some of it when you were in the present. Each new trial or whirlpool makes a bigger and bigger difference between past and future. So what you learn keeps increasing, making a bigger difference between past and future."

The boy stopped reading and typing. He thought he'd talked too much. He'd used too many words. He wasn't exactly sure of his logic. He had doubts. He looked up at The Man. He felt peace radiating from him. The Man soothed his fears.

"You know what I notice?" said the boy. "The professor uses bigger, more cerebral words like you do. They're like what a learned person would use. If you know the big words, it makes understanding the concepts easier to grasp.

"I just used a lot of big words. Using these kinds of learned words makes me feel self-conscious. I remember my dad saying to me, 'What are you, one of those eggheads from Harvard?'"

Dialogue Forty-Three
Science Leads to Justice of the Wise

The boy started making excuses for himself. Memories of his dad made him feel worthless. His abuse still lingered in the back of his mind. He looked The Man in the eye with false bravado and rationalized to justify his behavior. He'd learned that phrase in his senior psychology class. Even that phrase didn't stop him from being angry and abusive.

"I like to use shorter words that are like the conventional words that people use on the street in the poor sections. It takes twice as many words for me to say the same thing as an educated person. I'm not as exact. It seems so easy to challenge the conventional wisdom of my words, especially when the words I say are not explaining the thoughts that are in my head. My words seem so dull."

Being angry mixed up his words. He yelled at himself, *Get fired up! Learn, baby, learn!*

He was seeking another compliment. He waited for The Man to say something. The Man was silent. The boy didn't know how to fill the silence. Eventually, he spoke, saying things he thought The Man wanted to hear. "Your words are influential, the evidence of wisdom. When you talked to the Sadducees and Pharisees, you used powerful, authoritative words. They got mad at you because they feared you. In the end they tried to use your words against you."

The boy started using words to bring himself to the center of attention. He was feeling sorry for himself. "I like to use slang words. They can be trashy and tricky. I use stinging, sarcastic words. I talk trash. I'm crass. I attach strong emotions to my words, and they usually hurt people's feelings. So, people don't listen to me. They don't pay attention to what I mean. People get tired of me because they think I'm dim-witted and stupid. I use dumb words. That was another excuse for my dad to beat on me. He did crossword puzzles. I thought he was smart. But he rejected me. Just as other people rejected me."

"Get over it!" The Man retorted. "Quit feeling sorry for yourself. You are bigger than that! You can learn to think and feel like a person who is worthy of praise. Don't spoil it. Do you hear these clichés? What are you really learning?"

"I'm learning that your words demonstrate power, omnipotence. You use words that illustrate knowledge, omniscience." He knew he couldn't fool The Man. The boy paused.

The Man was watching him intently, waiting. The Man listened and gave his undivided attention to the boy. He knew the boy conversed within himself. He liked hearing himself talk. The boy thought he had to explain his behavior to please The Man. The boy was searching for the words of truth. He was clearing his conscience and coming into the light. He was philosophizing again. His soliloquies were becoming a frequent event. The Man waited for the exact moment to help the boy understand his behavior. He knew the boy was obstinate. The wait was worthwhile because the boy suddenly made a leap of faith.

"I hunger for righteousness as my most wanted beatitude. I think I understand righteousness as a virtue. It's behaving honestly, lawfully, and fairly by forms of justice. Most people are righteous. Being tactful, forgiving, and polite are acts of justice. These are behaviors of an enlightened or wise person. These are the deeds of Solomon. I want them! See, I did use some of your highbrow words."

The Man interrupted. "You are so right. The fear you have is the painful feeling of impending injustice. You determine that people are going to hurt you; that they are treating you unfairly, like a lowbrow. You feel they are going to reject you. Therefore, you use trash, crassness, and sarcasm to attack first."

This was a revelation for the boy. The concept of cause and effect was now clear. "Am I being a determinist like Einstein?" the boy asked. "Thinking like Einstein can't be all that bad. Unless it's bad, prejudiced, biased, narrow-minded determinism. Yeah, I understand!"

"Read what the professor wrote as it applies to injustice," The Man directed.

The boy logged on to his computer and read the words on the screen aloud. "The professor maintained that the more we know about our universe, the more difficult it becomes to believe in determinism. We live in an evolutionary universe whose roots lie in the fundamental laws of physics. We are now able to identify through the concept of instability, associated with deterministic chaos and nonintegrability, chance or probability as part of a new extended rationality. We established the mathematical theory of chaos.'"[83]

The Man said, "Can you explain to me, using your toy boat, what the professor wrote as it applies to you?"

"Well," the boy said, trying to mimic The Man, "the boat is going with the flow of the creek, and things are constantly changing. Learning the language of physics, we can describe the changes in our world, and we can adapt to steer the boat safely. If we also establish the mathematical language of chaos, we can reduce our doubts. Believing in strict determinism is an injustice to the truth.

"We can intellectually use the concepts of instability, deterministic chaos, integration, odds, and statistics. We can then put these concepts to work by the rationality of good scientific experiments. We can ease the painful feeling of impending danger or evil. Our data and information don't have to be one hundred percent deterministically perfect. We can be omniscient." The boy took a breath, smiled, and read some more of the professor's words mixed with his.[84]

"The fundamental laws of physics increase our abilities to create technologies that are more sophisticated. We can increase our computing power and know what is in the medium. This knowledge helps us with the dangers and evils of different diseases. The sciences of biology, genetics, medicine, and health care reduce our fear of the unknown. We become the knower of the physical sciences of chemistry, engineering, and architecture. Knowledge helps to satisfy our primary, belonging, secondary, and covert needs. Computing power, knowledge, understanding, and truth leads to justice of the wise."[85]

Dialogue Forty-Four
Computing Power

The boy paused and reflected for the longest time. The Man watched patiently. The boy started typing into his computer furiously. The Man waited. Finally, the boy spoke the words he had written.

"The greatest injustice and the most painful distress I feel is when children are abused and not helped to fulfill their beatitudes, destinies, and gifts of the Holy Spirit. God's will is for us to learn and adapt. We must strive to be enlightened and wise. Determinism is a narrow-minded way of thinking.

"God is omniscient, omnipotent, omnipresent, and beneficence. We must duplicate his traits and fulfill our own. We love others as we learn to love ourselves. This is justice. Love is the ultimate emotion. We can measure love by 'unto others'"

The Man had that charming glimmer in his eyes. He gently patted the boy on the back. "It brings pleasure to my heart when you believe in the concepts of omnipotence, omnipresence, omniscience, and beneficence. You are showing an understanding of the works of the Father. Go to your computer. Let us see what you have transferred from the medium to your hard drive."

The boy read from the screen. "Professor Ilya Prigogine asked another question: 'What are the roots of time?'" The boy then paraphrased the professor's answer and mixed in his own words.[86] "The answer to the question is: We are actually the children of the arrow of time, of evolution, not its progenitors. Wait!" yelled the boy, interrupting himself. "I didn't understand this when I first typed it."

Clarifying for the boy, The Man said, "Progenitor means a beginner, a direct ancestor or a forefather." The Man paused. The boy took over.

"I can't be an ancestor or forefather. No living thing can be a beginner and come before the arrow of time. We're too young. We don't have the power."

The Man interjected the professor's words: "'Humans as well as all other living things are evolving. As long as the sun is shinning and giving off energy, you are the children of the arrow of time. You can be orderly. You can make things. You can help other living things and yourself grow. You can change to something new. Humans are part of the arrow of time. They are surely not the roots of time.'"[87]

The boy and Man both became silent. They looked at each other.

The boy felt in perfect harmony with The Man. He broke eye contact with The Man and looked away, not wanting a challenge. He focused on the professor's words: "'Coherence due to irreversible, non-equilibrium processes makes life on Earth possible.'"[88] The boy pondered the words. He then talked to The Man about his interpretation.

"What if I said that coherence means sticking together, united, as parts of the same stuff. Therefore, when Humpty had all his parts together, he was a whole egg. He was programmed to be an egg, so he couldn't reverse the process and become the chicken he came from, but he could grow into a chicken in the future, if he didn't fall. It's like the past and future in the toy boat; they don't balance."

"Your words are okay."

The boy returned to his reading aloud: "'Chance, or probability, is no longer a convenient way of accepting ignorance, but rather part of a new, extended rationality. The professor considers the big bang an irreversible process par excellence. This irreversibility would result from instability in the pre-universe, induced by the interactions of gravitation and matter.'"[89]

The Man nodded his head for the boy to continue.

"'A succession of surprises arose. Scientists proved that Einstein's universe was so unstable that the smallest fluctuation would destroy it. Standard models help us understand what happened a fraction of a second after the birth of the universe. To give an idea of the values involved when we extrapolate back to the past, we come to a point of infinite density. Max Planck created some scales to measure the length, time, and energy obtained by using three universal constants: h, G, and c,'"[90] the boy said proudly. "I did the math, and the numbers are really, really small."

The boy locked eyes with The Man. Both The Man and the boy had a sparkle that revealed success. There was no challenge.

"I think I understand the professor's words without translating them," the boy continued. "We have paraphrased his statement many times. He agrees that our ability to find solutions to more difficult mathematical problems is dependent on our computing power. We can say it another way: as our computing power increases, so will our ability to find solutions to the more difficult mathematical problems. The hard drives on our computers resemble God's medium.

"The professor has also written words explaining his ideas about time, energy, and solving problems. The scientific world has accepted his words. I accept his words as true. He may not be a prophet of God; however, I think his words are sweeter than honey."

Dialogue Forty-Five
The Poem by a Prophet Poet

The boy began a new exchange of ideas between The Man and himself. "The Professor wrote,[91] 'The laws of nature no longer deal with certitudes but with possibilities. This disorder constitutes an evolutionary description associated with the second law of increasing entropy. Denying temporal succession, denying the arrow of time, denying the self, and denying the astronomical universe are apparent desperations and secret consolations.'"

The boy was excited with the way the knowledge was making sense. He remembered The Man explaining stereotypes, prejudices, biases, and keeping an open mind. "I'm learning a lot. I would like to make some definite statements of my own. This is what I think and what I feel in words. I do understand that God's words and languages are sweeter than honey," he said excitedly. "They truly are for the heart, mind, and soul. I'm a child of God, learning to overcome abuse." *Get fired up!*

The boy's passion was obvious. "I understand that words bring forth feelings and emotions from the heart. They bring forth ideas from the mind." The passion he was expressing carried over. "They bring forth values from the soul."

The Man reflected on how much the boy needed praise. He still feared rejection. The Man knew his job was to separate the boy's natural gift of intelligence from pride, arrogance, and narcissism. Humility must saddle the boy's gift of being smart. The boy was warming up to present another of his soliloquies. The Man allowed the boy the freedom to express his newfound knowledge.

The boy started. "Words and language are not just for the mind, the intellect, or for 'appearances' sake. No matter what words I say or hear, the words themselves elicit feelings, emotions, actions, or behaviors. I learned a child's rhyme that said, 'Sticks and stones will break my bones, but names will never hurt me.' This is not true. Names do hurt. The rhyme was just a way of pretending you could block out the bad words.

"I'm beginning to see that all words are sweeter than honey. All

God's languages and words are sweeter than honey. It's how you use them that makes them sweet or sour, good or bad. The fear of God is pure. The sin of overweening pride, an act of insensate pride brought God's wrath at the Tower of Babel against their one language."

"Your words and ideas are excellent," said The Man.

The boy accepted the praise. He blushed a subtle shade of pink. "So I must remember that I catch more flies with honey than I do with vinegar. The professor's words are sweeter than honey. There is no denying the meaning of his scientific language. How's that for a starter for catching a fly?"

The boy was in his usual position, sitting with his computer in his lap. He looked up at The Man. He was hesitant asking The Man's permission to bring up another topic. "Can I add something?"

The Man smiled and said, "What if I were to say no? Work on being humble instead. Would you still want to bring up a new topic?"

A startled gaze came over his face, and the boy stared at The Man. He then saw that The Man's smile had changed, and He let out to a hearty laugh. "Are you making fun of me?" the boy countered.

The Man continued to laugh, reacting with a laughing nod. "Hey, my little big man, lighten up! Be cool. Intensity slows you down. Go ahead, tell me about your new topic."

"Yeah, okay, I get your drift. I know I get pretty serious and intense when I'm learning something new. I do get focused! Well, anyway, I read this poem I want to share with you, and it's pretty intense. It was so intense that it scared me. I think I understand the symbolic meanings. Let's say it is a poem by a prophet poet. I don't know the author. However, it is his or hers to claim. The words are sweeter than honey." He quoted what the prophet poet had written:

Time is the substance of which I am made. Time is a river, which sweeps me along, but I am a river; Time is a tiger, which destroys me, but I am a tiger; Time is a fire, which consumes me; but I am a fire. The world, fortunately, is real; I, unfortunately, am me. Time and reality are irreducibly linked. Denying Time may be either a consolation or a triumph of human reason. Denying Time is always a negation of reality.

The boy waited. Finally, he spoke. "Well, what do you think of the poem?"

Dialogue Forty-Six
The Meaning of the Poem

The Man had his index finger on his nose, with his thumb under his chin. He nodded his head slowly. He was in deep thought. He was intently watching the teenage boy, who was rapidly growing into a man. Finally, he spoke to the boy. "Do you think there is some trick to the poem?"

The boy's eyes flashed open, not clear what The Man was referring to. The Man explained.

"People use words and language to market products and spin words to give exaggerated meanings. Be on guard of the con man. You do remember that your dad told you to be leery of perverts. So when we read poetry or listen to conversations, we give it one hundred percent of our effort. At that moment, we believe with all our minds and hearts as to the obvious meaning, also paying attention to what, if any, the hidden or implied meaning is. Reading poetry is an excellent teacher."

"No," the boy replied, "I don't think the prophet poet was trying to trick us. If anything, I think the poet was using words and languages sweeter than honey to get us to analyze and believe."

He paused, waiting for a response from The Man. The Man did nothing. The boy explained his ideas.

"The words are for the heart, mind, and soul. As I read the words, they brought forth my feelings and emotions." He looked up at The Man for a sign and continued. "They brought forth ideas from my mind. They brought forth values from my soul. Is using too many words bad?"

"You use learned words along with your slang to express some profound ideas. That is okay between us. Explain to me your interpretation of the poem."

The boy tried to think in only learned words. "I think the chemist and the poet come close to proving with their words the existence of the Father, Son, and Holy Spirit. Their languages make this possible.

"I now realize that all laws, whether moral or natural, are not absolute. They are probabilities, possibilities, and uncertainties based on statistics. The chemist uses the probabilistic language of the natural scientific laws of the universe; the poet uses words for the heart, soul, and mind of believers. Neither language is absolute."

The boy withdrew within himself. The Man recognized the fright the boy was feeling. The boy spoke his words slowly, just above a whisper, and looked around furtively. "Do you remember when I heard words echoing in my heart and head? What a dumb question. Of course you remember." With each word, his voice got louder. "The words scared me, almost giving me a heart attack. Let me tell you—I was scared!

"I'll never forget them. The words were vividly printed on my very being. They were soothing and calm, yet authoritative. They were slow and melodious in delivery yet mysteriously powerful." He continued, raising his voice. "I am! I am the Word! I am the Logos! I have no beginning or end. I am Time! I have no age! I can communicate with everything at the same instant in the arrow of time. I can talk to the heart, soul, and mind of everyone." The boy stopped. He let out his breath.

"Boy! Those words still bring chills up and down my spine after all this time." It took a while for the boy to relax. Finally, the boy said calmly, "When I compare the poet's words, 'Time is the substance of which I am made,' to the scary words, especially 'I am Time,' I know that the poet is saying that we are made of the same stuff as God.

"The poet declared, 'Time is a river, which sweeps me along, but I am a river.' He is saying that the Father is the universe. The universe is a river surging in the arrow of time. Each person is his or her own entity that exists as a small river; most of us are like little boats flowing in a creek. All waters eventually combine with the Father."

The Man couldn't help himself. He had to praise the boy. "Little big man, you have one fantastic imagination. So far, your interpretation is right on. A creek, brook, or stream is just as important as a river. Please excuse the interruption," The Man apologized.

The boy started to swell up with pride. Then he remembered to put on his saddle of humility. "The poet stated, 'Time is a tiger, which destroys me, but I am a tiger.' Here he is saying that the Father has the same feelings and emotions we do. They can destroy you. The animal in you, with its feelings and emotions controlled for selfish, insensate pride, is a vicious tiger. With its feelings and emotions expressed properly, it is a beautiful tiger.

"The poet expressed, 'Time is a fire, which consumes me, but I am a fire.' He is saying the Father has ambitious aspirations for the mind and soul of humans. The fire is the Holy Spirit. The achievements of the intellect can consume us. Humans must learn to anneal the ambitious aspirations of the mind and soul with the aid of the Holy Spirit."

The boy paused, then continued, "The poet voiced solemnly, 'the world, fortunately, is real; I, unfortunately, am me.' He is saying that the Father has created a real universe. It has real moral and natural laws. They are not exact or absolute. There are limitations to their systems of language. Unfortunately, we must exist within these uncertainties. We have to live with our gifts. We have the freedom of a challenging conscience.

"The poet asserts that 'time and reality are irreducibly linked.' Here he is saying that the Father and the universe are one. They are what are real. We struggle with the understanding of this reality.

"The poet's truism, 'Denying Time may be either a consolation or a triumph of human reason,' is saying that denying the Father is yours to decide with your mind. However, your heart and soul, with their feelings and emotions, still yearn to have a connection with the ultimate love of the Father.

"The poet's final truism is this: 'Denying Time is always a negation of reality.' He is saying that denying the Father is denying the moral and natural laws of the universe.

"We already read what the professor wrote."

The laws of nature no longer deal with certitudes but with possibilities. This disorder constitutes an evolutionary description associated with the second law, the law of increasing entropy. Denying temporal succession, denying the arrow of time, denying the self, and denying the astronomical universe are apparent desperations and secret consolations."

The boy began a pompous soliloquy. One thing he'd learned from being abused was that he acted out instantly with emotion. "The prophet poet and the professor use different forms of communication.

Yet they can agree. Since the Tower of Babel, the intention is to have many languages; they also can agree. However, the people denied and rejected the Creator. They had their intellect, their reasons. This stubborn stance did not satisfy the hearts, minds, and souls of the people.

"The Father sent you, my Man, to redeem the denial and rejection. The people abused, tortured, and crucified You. Please excuse my bluntness, but the memory of my abuse keeps coming back in my nightmares. Lately the memory explodes on me during my waking moments. It's scary!"

With all the humility a teenage boy could gather, he stepped over to The Man, buried his face in The Man's neck, wrapped his arms around The Man's back, and hugged as strongly as he could. The Man returned the embrace.

CHAPTER EIGHT
An eighteen-year-old boy learns about laws

Dialogue Forty-Seven
Obeying the Orders

The Man gently cradled the boy's head to His neck with His hand. The boy was getting angry. He could feel the rage building up within as he remembered the sadistic abuse by his father. The hatred of The Man's Crucifixion and His violent pain and fear brought torrents of tears. He sobbed the words: "You taught me that all humanity rejected the Father, and we've been deaf to him ever since. If we weren't, we'd hear him."

He kept sobbing as he spoke. "Most of the time, my own listening is garbled by insignificant thoughts going around in my head." He paused and sobbed. He was feeling shame. "Do we pay attention to another's conversation?" His sobbing was overpowering. "I don't think we truly listen to people and what they are saying." The guilt was piling up inside his chest. "I think we are only waiting for a talker to pause or take a breath so we can interject our own thoughts." His sobbing was uncontrollable.

"You said, 'We are so deadened to His voice, because of the rationality of our intellect. We just take facts and make up a story that fits them.'" Aiming his anger at himself, he took a couple of deep breaths and continued. "You said, 'He speaks to our feelings and emotions.' However, that is too easy. I know you couldn't hate us, but you surely were resentful." He tilted his head back to look up at The Man's face. "I know I have doubts. I have even said that God doesn't exist."

The Man gently pushed the boy away from His chest. Holding the boy tenderly by the shoulders, He stared intently into the boy's eyes. He demanded in a loud voice:

I order you to memorize this statement. Are you ready? The master who believes he understands his slaves because they obey his orders would be intolerant and blind. Now I insist that you rescind that order.

The boy heard these words; however, he had no clue as to their meaning. Was he listening? He wasn't sure. Had he memorized it? No, he remembered it had to do with masters, slaves, and obeying.

Someone was intolerant and blind. Was The Man mad at him? He was to rescind an order. He questioned which one to rescind, the order to memorize this statement; or the one to obey his orders; or the one to rescind that order.

The boy couldn't deal with memorizing statements when he was so flustered over the cruelty of the Crucifixion—or the hatred and evil of all the different forms of abuse. He was truly learning: to mourn the regretful events of abuse and crucifixion; to redeem denial and the rejection, The Man had allowed the Crucifixion. The boy felt the empathic anguish of The Man. The boy gazed at The Man through teary eyes, only to see the tears of sorrow rolling down The Man's cheeks.

The Man directed the grief of His Crucifixion toward the meaning of the poem. His heart ached not for the laws of science and the beauty of the creation, but for the use of scientific technology from biblical times to the present. The scientific imagination of humans created the whips, the nails, the cross, the swords, the weapons, the armaments, the chariots, the tanks, the planes, the bombs, and so forth. He spoke the next words aloud with passion, so the boy had to listen.

"The streams of science become a vicious, violent weapon, and nobody wins the battle with only our self-centered, insensate, prideful, and narcissistic emotions in control." The Man growled the words. "The tiger is on the prowl. The moral laws are out of control." The Man paused. The boy was gawking at Him.

"God becomes obsolete, and science wins the battle, with only the cold, mathematical intellect of logic intact and in control of the conscience. The Holy Spirit senses the rejection. The passionate fire of ambitious aspirations to do God's Will is drenched."

The Man fell silent. He raised His head and felt the warmth of the sun's light on His face and beard. He said, "The Father wins the battle when we are conscious of our emotions of fear, doubt, pain, guilt, love—and our value of right and wrong helps us make a clear, intelligent decision.

"Each waterway flows in peace. Each tiger preserves its forest. The passionate fire is used to anneal the mind to find its ambitious aspirations." As with any great orator, The Man used his pauses, inflections, and the softness and power of his voice to spellbind His audience. In this case, The Man enthralled the eighteen-year-old boy.

"The Father did not take away from us our emotions," said The Man. "He had me portray our emotions in the direst of moments. The complete control of our real emotions by others or ourselves can never be. Making slaves of our intellect or our emotions can never be. The master who believes he understands his intellect and emotions because they obey his orders would be intolerant and blind."

The boy thought about this last statement as the one he was supposed to memorize. There was a slight difference in the words. Yet he thought he got a much better gist of the meaning by what The Man just said.

The Man transferred from the prophet poet mode of language to the scientific style of language. "Mathematical equations describe complexities of the universe with accuracy. Shrouded in a veil of self-righteous intellectualism by the use of mathematics, divorced from the heart, science with its esoteric knowledge of, for example, antimatter arrives in this world with no ethical instructions. Science obeys its master. It can spread like a cancer. The Internet connects us to all areas of the earth. It is a rational experience being online and sharing data, information, ideas, and knowledge. The technology that promises to unite us must do so. The technology of science may sanctify its miracles. Science can save us from our needs of hunger, safety, shelter, and sickness.

"Feelings are difficult to share, leaving us to feel alone no matter what emotions are aroused in the private moments of being with another, or even being online."

The boy was beginning to understand why The Man ordered him to memorize the statement that had to do with his intellect and emotions being slaves. We can't make emotions or intellect our slaves. Nor can we let them get the best of us. The boy marveled at The Man going into His scholarly speech to get him out of his crying jag. The boy spoke the words aloud as he typed them into his computer.

"Always available for the asking, The Man is an excellent coach to teach us the medium. The model of the Tower of Babel, with only one language, is not acceptable. The Man can teach us the languages of our emotions and intellect. The Holy Spirit brings the fire of ambitious aspirations to do the will of the Father, and understand through our intellect. The tiger is the animal in us, our feelings and emotions. We flow in our creeks or streams to the river. Time is the love of the universe, a river surging in the arrow of time. Time and reality link irreducibly. The Father, the Son, and The Holy Spirit. This is the team."

Dialogue Forty-Eight
The Man Was Human

He spoke to The Man. "You are absolutely the best teacher! You taught me that we destroy our self-worth as human beings when we do not fulfill the essence of who we are. Prophets and poets describe the wonderful emotional beauty of our universe. We cannot allow science to proclaim that planet Earth and its inhabitants are a meaningless speck in the grand scheme.

"You said that skepticism with its doubting attitude questions the truth of knowledge and can hinder false growth. It can also aid in the freedom of true growth. So, skepticism works both ways.

"You taught me that cynicism demands proof with a sarcastic denial of the goodness of human motives. We need only open our minds to hear the wisdom of cynicism. It is also about virtues being the only good. It also works both ways. Each of us contributes as a cynic."

The Man cut in with His third statement about the master and the slaves: "The master who believes he understands his *virtues* and *vices* because they obey his orders would be intolerant and blind. Did you memorize, understand, and rescind the order? Now I want you to rescind that order," He demanded.

The boy stared at The Man, totally bewildered. His imagination was running wild. Was The Man acting like a coldhearted human being? Or was it as if The Man were on a stage giving the oration of His life? This time was different from His big bang vocalization. The boy was awestruck. The Man's commanding presence demanded that you heard, felt, and understood every little detail of the message about the order. He was being human in every aspect. He was standing. His arms stretched open and wide in a supplicating manner were calling the boy to come forth.

The Man's magnetic charisma captivated the boy. It was weird. The boy's thoughts were about the history of The Man and his people. Deep inside his subconscious, the boy compared Moses to The Man. Moses spoke with God face-to-face and then conveyed the law to the chosen people. Following Moses were the prophets of the Historical Books. In the Wisdom literature, God reveals his face only in Israel. To the Jews, God is law. They are in a juridical relationship with God.

The Jews found it extremely difficult to convert from the law God to the greater God, the God of love. This would not mean giving up their obedience, but rather that this obedience would flow from deeper wellsprings. To obey would be their choice of free will. Obedience would be bigger in scope and fairness, more open, pure, and humble, with a cherished freedom. The law came through Moses. He was a man.

The boy felt his subconscious bubble up and compare The Man to something unbelievably profound. The Man was also a Man like Moses. Yet He was more. He was being godlike in every aspect. Grace, love, and truth came through The Man. He brought God unveiled. He brought to each person His communion of will with the Father. His fulfillment of all righteousness opens heaven, which is essentially the place where God fulfills His will perfectly. Sated, the boy fell asleep.

The morning sunlight was sprinkling through the canopy of leaves on the trees. The boy looked up, thinking the sun's emission was the light The Man brought to everyone. The rays were the symbol of God. The sun's heat warmed him. The energy gave him a warm, fuzzy feeling as he thought he heard The Man saying, "Anyone who does the will of the Father in Heaven is my brother sister and mother."[92] The boy listened to The Man in his imagination. He fell back asleep, dreaming he was to unite his will with the will of The Man—trying to accomplish in his heart the obedience intended by the Torah. The Man is the Torah, the law as the Word of God in person.

The boy dreamed. A prophet's destiny was to emulate The Man. The message of the prophets meant not worldly power but the cross—and the radically different community through the cross. The Man is not a master that you have to obey blindly. He is more than obedience to the laws. He's watchful and tolerant. He's not bossy!

The boy was still half-asleep. He knew he was dreaming. It seemed like an eternity had passed since they first sat in their usual place under the trees in the shade. Learning the words about math, science, and laws ad infinitum satiated the boy's storehouse of accumulated information.

Understanding the bottom line for a person's destiny is to discover the laws and to be responsible for their use. He dreamed of his challenge to put all this information into some form of organized knowledge. He knew this applied to both natural and moral laws. He dreamed this was the right thing to do. It would be hard work; he just finished his first year of college. *Be positive! Get fired up! Multitask!*

The Man standing over him and stretching down to tap his shoulder interrupted the boy's dream. *Nah!* he thought. *The laws can wait! What's the word? Procrastination. Yeah! That's it! The laws can wait till a rainy day. The sun feels so good! I could lie here all day. A second year of college can wait.* He rolled over and tried to go back to sleep.

The Man reached down and pulled the boy to his feet. He woke up with a start! "You're it!" yelled The Man, as He tapped the boy on the head. The boy was still drowsy. They played a game like tag. The boy became wide-awake. The Man let the boy tackle Him. They rolled and wrestled in the mulch. They jumped up and ran into the morning sunlight. Their jogging attained a nice rhythmic gait with deep breathing. After a while, The Man asked a question.

"Would you like to hear the story of how Paul preached to the Romans and Galatians about the laws?"

The boy made a wry face. The boy was full up to his eyebrows with words about laws. So he yelled ironically, "Oh, yeah!" He cheered sardonically and applauded with a contemptuous slow cadence. He shouted his phony approval: "All right, bring on 'em laws."

Little did the boy realize that this included learning more about the laws in-depth. The Man expected him to work his hardest.

The Man roared with laughter. The boy's behavior delighted Him. One minute he was sleepy and moping around. In the next, he was overwhelmed with information and obstinate. In the next, his curiosity was piqued and he wanted more.

Dialogue Forty-Nine
Paul and the Galatians about Laws[93]

The Man knew how to teach the laws and help the boy have fun learning them at the same time. The key was in storing the information into knowledge clumps to be recalled and used later.

"First," The Man directed, "we imagine Paul standing in the center of a portico, a porch, attached to a large building. It has six slim Greek sculptured statues supporting the roof, leaving three sides open to an audience in the semicircular atrium. Can you picture this in your imagination?" The Man and boy continued running as The Man described the clumps of knowledge.

"Second, Paul is a great orator. We know of the oral and written sources he used. We know his ways of expressing himself. His voice carried magnificently to his listeners.

"Third, the portico is designed as a perfect place to preach. It focuses the sound on the listeners.

"Fourth, here's the setting. I will take the role of Paul, with all his mannerisms.

"Fifth," The Man continued, "your imagination will see Me act out his character as if I were Paul. I will take on the persona of Paul and speak in Paul's voice.

"Sixth, you will be his listeners. You can shout, yell, or improvise your role in our story. You will refer to the Bible, chapter, and verse in the computer, but we will not say them aloud.

"Seventh, we want this story to be about Paul and his preaching about the law. We know the era in which he lived. He knew the languages of Aramaic, Hebrew, and Hellenistic Greek. He was well versed in the law.

"Eighth, Paul is determined to correct the Jews' proud reliance on the law.

"Ninth, some fundraising Christians who had visited the Galatians advised the gentile converts to be circumcised. They preached that circumcision ensured their salvation. This would have meant adopting all the prescriptions of the law.

"Tenth, the implications of which, to Paul, made nonsense of Christ's redemptive work.

"Eleventh, it was for this reason that Paul opposed the circumcision of his converts so violently. He maintained that the true value of the law could be appreciated only by seeing the place of circumcision in the development of God's plan.

"Twelve, this is the plot for Paul in our story. The law was the monitor until Christ came to bring about justification through faith. To us acting as the Galatians, I will use literary forms to paraphrase the words of Paul to modern-day words so we can understand what he meant."

The Man bowed and projected His voice to his imaginary audience of playgoers. Thus, He began His impersonation of the orator apostle, Paul. His voice rang out!

The Mosaic Law is good and holy because it reveals God's will to the Jews. We Jews were locked in the law without having the spiritual power necessary to obey it; all the law could do was make people aware of sin and of the need they have for God to help them.

The boy and his imaginary listeners shouted, "Hear the words, listen up! Come on, Paul, tell us more!" They swayed, clapped, and danced.

The Man moved stage right. He continued in Paul's voice:

All human beings need this help, and it is necessarily a gift from God: it was promised to Abraham long before the law was formulated and has now been given.

"Oh yeah! Think positive! Come on, Paul, tell us more!" called the listeners. They increased the tempo of their dance.

The Man, as Paul, spoke:

In Jesus, His death and resurrection have destroyed the old humanity, which was corrupted by Adam's sin, and created a new humanity of which Christ himself is the prototype.

"Hey, Paul! Come on, Paul, tell us more!" the boy added. "Way to go, Paul!" Their bodies moved in time to their clapping.

The Man returned to center stage and spoke:

All human beings, united to Christ by faith, and living a new life by sharing the Spirit of Christ, without any merit on their part, are made upright and enabled to carry out God's will. We live united to Christ by faith!

The boy realized that only brothers were in the crowd. "Right on, brothers!" They bopped to the same rhythm. "Awesome! Have faith! Come on, Paul, tell about faith!" The crowd swayed.

The Man moved stage left and spoke:

This faith must result in good works, but these good works will not be at all the same as those good works commanded by the law, on which Jews were so proud to rely; they will be works prompted by the presence of the Spirit.

"Get fired up! Get fired up! Come, O Holy Spirit!" The crowd was one body.

The Man returned to center stage and spoke again:

It can be done by all who have faith, Jews or gentiles.

"Way to go! We are brothers!" The crowd swayed and bopped.

The Man stayed at center stage, saying:

The preparatory or Mosaic stage of religion is over, and Jews who claim they are continuing to fulfill the law are, in fact, putting themselves outside the pale of salvation. One day all Jews will become believers.

"Be positive! The Mosaic is over! Way to go! We will all be brothers in faith!"

The Man walked the stage, continuing to speak:

All converts must love and help one another as one family. We will be one in the family! We will be one in Christ!

"Get fired up! Love one another! We will all be brothers in faith! The family is the way to go. We will be one in family! We will be one in Christ."

156 James J. McBride Ph.D.

Dialogue Fifty
Paul and the Romans about Faith[94]

The Man, as Paul, waited until he had his imaginary listeners' undivided attention. At that moment, He yelled at them:

How did you receive the Spirit? Through the law or through faith?

The boy responded as if he were all the listeners. "Huh!" He was dumbfounded. The Man continued His diatribe:

How could you be so stupid? After beginning in the spirit, then ending in the flesh, have you had remarkable experiences all to no purpose—if indeed they were to no purpose? Is it because you have faith in what you heard that God lavishes the Spirit on you and works wonders in your midst?

The Man softened his performance as Paul spoke lovingly to the Galatians:

Abraham believed God, and God gave him faith as justice. Scripture saw in advance that God's way of justifying the Gentiles would be through faith. All who believe are blessed along with Abraham, The Man of faith.

The boy's senses started working again. He felt the fire of his ambitious aspirations.

All who depend on the law are under a curse. No one is justified in God's sight by the law, for the just Man shall live by faith. The law's terms are, 'Whoever does these things shall live by them.'

The Man again hesitated, feeling the pain of the Crucifixion. The boy was sensitive to The Man's pain.

Christ has delivered us from the power of the law's curse by himself becoming a curse for us. Accursed is anyone who is hanged on a tree.

The blessing bestowed on Abraham descends on us in Jesus, making it possible for us to receive the promised Spirit through faith.

There were promises spoken to Abraham and to his 'descendant—Christ'. A covenant ratified by God is not set aside as invalid by any law that came into being later, nor is its promise nullified. The promise God granted Abraham is his privilege. It is unthinkable to mean that the law is opposed to the promises of God.

The true function of the law is justice. However, Scripture has locked all things in under the constraint of sin. Why? So the promise might be fulfilled in those who believe in the true function of faith in Jesus.

Annealing his ambitious aspirations for The Man, the boy felt as if the Holy Spirit jolted him by the fire.

The Man continued his oration.

Before faith came, we were under the constraint of the law, locked in until the faith that was coming should be revealed. The law was our monitor until Christ came to bring about our justification through faith.

The boy knew that his highest aspirations were to have The Man as his father, The Man as his teacher, and The Man as his friend. He would learn the laws, both moral and natural. They would guide him. However, he could rescind them if they steered his boat into rivers with eddies of ill repute. Follow The Man. It's a win-win!

The Man began to bellow:

All who receive circumcision are bound to the law in its entirety. Any of you who seek your justification in the law have severed yourselves from Christ and fallen from God's favor!

In the Spirit, we eagerly await the justification we hope for, and only faith can yield it. By means of the gift of love, place yourselves at one another's service. The whole law has found its fulfillment in this one saying: 'You shall love your neighbor as yourself.'

If you go on biting and tearing one another to pieces, take care! You will end up in mutual destruction!

Live in accord with the Spirit and you will not yield to the cravings of the flesh of abused emotions. Abused emotions lust against the Spirit, and the Spirit against abused emotions; they are opposed. If you are guided by the Spirit, you are not under the misused power of the laws.

The boy yelled, "Yeah! Get fired up! Come, O Holy Spirit!"

The Man moved around on the stage, and with a low, angry voice spoke:

The flesh is lewd conduct, impurity, licentiousness, idolatry, sorcery, hostilities, bickering, jealousy, and outbursts of rage, selfish rivalries, dissensions, and factions. Engaging behaviors of envy, drunkenness, orgies, and the like, will not permit you to inherit the Kingdom of God.

In contrast, the fruit of the Spirit is love, joy, peace, patient endurance, kindness, generosity, faith, mildness, and chastity. Against such, there is no law!

To love Me is to crucify your flesh with its passions and desires to misuse power. Live by the Spirit and follow the Spirit's lead. Never be boastful or challenging, or jealous toward one another.

The demands of conscience are to live by the Spirit and help others do the same. Look to your own conduct. Bear your own responsibility. Be instructed in the Word and share all with God. No one makes a fool of God. Do not grow weary of doing good. Have faith.

The Man asked the boy, "Did you receive the Spirit?"

Dialogue Fifty-One
Write Using Different Words, Languages, and Styles

The boy was extremely excited. His brain was on overload. In addition, he was emotionally exhausted. With a tired voice, he replied, "Yes, I received the Spirit!"

He started a new conversation as he sat down under the umbrella of trees. "I cherished Your performance as Paul. You were perfect. I believed in you! You so love everything you do. Yeah! What else is new. Paul's words are so eloquent. I did not have to imagine Paul's delivery. You were Paul. But Paul's words are so complicated. He uses many words in long sentences. I get confused. But you made it easier for me to understand."

The boy continued his critical remarks. "Law is not my thing. I can't talk law! It is like math and physics; you have to study hard to understand the meaning. But, math and science give better answers. They're more exact. Laws are like chaos; like running into an eddy; if you change something a little bit, it changes the whole argument."

A long pause followed. Finally, the Boy brought up the topic he was interested in talking about. "Our last fifteen Dialogues have been serious work. The words are harder and bigger. The sentences are longer and more complicated. The themes and concepts are at a higher level of abstraction.

"Last Christmas, Maribel, my cousin, gave me a wonderful book by David Gregory.[95] I don't want to plagiarize anyone's language or ideas, so I suggest you read his book. I would just like all the authors to be part of the team with You, my Man, as the coach. Will you coach me so I can learn to write using many different words, languages, and styles? I want to learn to express my opinion about being religious in a religion."

The Man's eyes glowed. He tilted his head slightly to the side and looked down at the boy with that enigmatic smile on his face. "Is there a little eddy spinning your boat?" he teased. "All right, I'll help, but you are gonna pay for this. I'll expect a lot of love and respect. You had better be ready to pay up! How many 'unto others' do you have?" He was pulling the boy's leg.

His smile turned to laughter as He jumped up into the crouched stance of a western gunslinger, pointing his finger at the boy with his thumb cocked upward. "Just remember," He said in Western slang, "when you point your index finger and accuse someone, the lower three fingers are pointing back at you." He then said as an afterthought, "You are not plagiarizing." He blew on His finger, blowing away the imaginary smoke. He tucked His finger under His robe.

To the boy, it was strange to see The Man playact a gunslinger. *Hmmm,* thought the boy. *I guess a gunslinger pointing a gun is like accusing or judging someone with words and disparagingly pointing your finger.*

The boy interrupted his own thoughts by saying to The Man, "Aren't you teaching me that people are free? Free to enjoy being the children of God? You told me I was one of God's children. I was free—free to learn, free to grow as a human—to become a beautiful person as God intended. You said nobody could make this a law."

The Man nodded approval.

The boy's next questions were caustic. "Doesn't it make you sick when people in authority misuse their power? The boy answered for The Man with another question: "Yes?" When The Man stayed quiet, the boy became even more critical and sarcastic. "Well, let me tell You that being free is impossible in the presence of the rigid authority of church people. It's like they are abusive. How's that for words?

"Remember Mrs. Andrews … my teacher? Well, she and the church people are the same. They want to control everybody's thinking and curb free expression. I've only been around for nineteen years, but I know what it's like to be snubbed and abused as a nonperson.

"I remember last Easter when I went to church. The pastor tried right up to the end of the services to change the people's attitudes. He washed the feet of the make-believe apostles from the congregation. He told all in the congregation to be humble and serve rather than dominate and dictate. He wanted the church people to guide and manage, not to abuse, dictate, and legislate like those who govern the world. Although the pastor didn't use these exact words, he didn't dispel the tendency of his unbending authority to tell other people how to live.

"As soon as we got off our knees and out the door, most people were back being masters and bosses, dictating and abusing each other as slaves. They act as if they have to obey the rituals and rules preached to them. If they disobey or break a rule, that's okay—just go to confession and ask for forgiveness. Don't we ever envision masters and bosses in the worldly sense as the ultimate selfish abusers? How's that for words?"

The boy saw his outstretched arm and hand, with his finger pointing at The Man. He saw the other three lower fingers pointing back at him. He realized he was judging The Man and all others with the one finger, but the other three were judging him. What a hypocrite he was for judging the church people."

He spoke to The Man contritely. "You told me that the people in charge don't know how to love. They hurt without intending to because they know only law ... not love. You taught me that the laws are ruthless and unbending. They break people under the weight. You wanted to put people before the law. But there are so many laws. I have to obey the laws of churches, the laws of physics, and the laws of governments.

"I remember Your telling me that there's a big difference between the way religion is and the way God intended it to be. You said You came to Earth to try to free people from the kind of regimented religion where people are threatened if they don't obey rules and rituals and laws invented by the clergy. You said that can't be legislated."

The boy paused. He was trying to remember all the lessons The Man had taught him. He had just learned one on his own. Pointing fingers at others makes you a hypocrite. How could he be a skeptic or a cynic without being a hypocrite? *Hmmm,* he thought. *Can I do this without passing judgment on another person?*

CHAPTER NINE
A Nineteen year old boy
learns about Religions

Dialogue Fifty-Two
Religious Observance Rather Than God

The Man was watching him carefully as He took over. He spoke softly with sorrow in his voice and the boy listened carefully.

"One of our lessons was about the big difference between the way religion is and the way the Father intended it to be. We thought it to be essential that the apostles and the community act as a support to each other. They were to provide help. They were to enable and to console each other with love. They were to do 'unto others'. We sought the apostles to guide and serve, not to dictate and legislate like those who govern the world. We were especially concerned with hypocrisy.

"Unfortunately, religious leaders modeled themselves after politicians, civil governments and corporations: the presidents, VPs, CEOs, CFOs, COOs, and so on." The Man sadly reflected. "They created a chain of command; a line of authority from the highest to the lowest. They treated people accordingly, as underlings. This is the same trap that the Scribes, Sadducees and Pharisees fell into—making religion a tangible set of measurable religious observances, which is legalistic, superficial, and abusive to the intellect. It is the literal transference of the hypocrite's thoughts. Do what I say, not as I do.

"The apostles tried hard not to follow the same model. Over the years, the clergy made rules and laws for their own justification. The focus was on religious observance rather than love of the Father. Religions sought high ideals, but attached endless rules and rituals rather than a relationship based on the love of 'unto others.' The concern was to occupy the people's attention with customs, practices, rituals, and traditions. These replaced the true service of the Father and concern for positive acts of 'unto others.' The clergy were too stuck on their own authority to allow people to be free and to function as mature relating people. This was their hypocrisy. They could only pretend to have the character it takes to believe in a loving God. Their God was a God of rules and laws. A form of abuse to control by the power of law."

The boy couldn't wait to give his opinion on the subject. "In my computer I have the history of building cathedrals to the sky. Bishops in the twelve and thirteen hundreds tried to outbuild each other with bigger and taller cathedrals. Being religious meant worshiping at a church or cathedral by making a pilgrimage. I also have the idea that authentic worshipers will worship the Father in spirit, truth and do 'unto others.' Remember when we stopped at the well to get a drink. It was just as You did in olden times with the woman who had all the husbands. She wanted to believe and be authentic. Yet, many of the people were hypocritical about talking to a Samaritan woman.

"Hey, I just had another thought! In my work at the planetarium as a student assistant, we have a Power Point presentation on Stonehenge. Each year for the last three years, I have helped the director make minor changes in the presentation by adding new information. Stonehenge is a perfect example of how people begin a religion. May I tell you about it?" He looked at The Man for permission, because he'd used the word 'may' on purpose to see if He would allow it. When The Man gave him a big nod with a heart pleasing big smile, the boy almost jumped out of his skin with pleasure.

"Okay, here we go! Be positive get fire up! This will be my story, not the one we show at the planetarium. I want to exaggerate some things we leave out of the public presentation and make my own theory based on the same evidence, but it will be my interpretation. Can I do that?" asked the boy.

"Sure, why not," said The Man. "Have you ever thought what it would be like to be the first human beings to roam the earth with free will and the ability to have a spoken language? Let's say that this came about seventy thousand years ago. Use your imagination and think of the first things they'll do."

The boy was quiet for a long while, trying to form a picture in his head, and then he blurted out the words, "They'll have sex and make babies!" —His face turned a bright red showing his embarrassment. He didn't mind for his next words were just as strong.

The people will realize they have to feed each other so they can be strong enough to survive and have more babies. They'll have to build or find warm shelters when the babies are born. The men will hunt, and the women will gather food. They'll form a tribe. A mean leader takes over and beats his men, women, and children. A strong kid runs away and soon steals a woman from another tribe and forms his own tribe.

He's not mean, and he forms a viable tribe where the men and women work together as a team. He's a good leader. They grow prosperous and form a town with farms and animals." The boy stopped talking and reflected for a while so he could continue his story.

"Here's where the laws come in. The first laws would have to do with survival. There had to be enough food. The good leader watched the plants and animal grow and gained the knowledge of the seasons of the earth. The plants and animals started growing at the vernal equinox. The animals got fat and had many plants to eat during the summer solstice. The people harvested the food and slaughtered the animals at the autumnal equinox. They stored the food and prepared for the winter solstice. They followed the earth's pattern.

"They developed priesthoods who formulated more social and moral laws. The first astrologers watched the stars and the close correlation between the sun, moon, stars, and the earth's seasons to formulate the first scientific laws. The laws were more like oral traditions passed down from one generation to the next. The priests and astrologers started the first religions. They developed festivals, rituals, traditions, and orgies during the four seasons of the year. They learned about herbs, other special plants that healed, and some that killed. They mourned and found places to bury their dead. They learned about their waste and how to get rid of it. One achievement led to another.

"I'll refer to Stonehenge as one of the greatest achievements in the world. The mystery of Stonehenge is its many theories of how a culture produced a great achievement with no written language. Other first cultures did leave written records. Many aspects of Stonehenge remain subject to debate for lack of a written language. Was it built as an astronomical observatory or as a religious site? However, most present scientists concede that Stonehenge and the surrouding areas were probably multifunctional and used for ancestor worship as well. Our story continues with the priests and astrologers building a monument in honor of the earth's patterns to form their religion and to worship their dead.

"Stonehenge went through at least ten major phases over a period of two thousand years. It was first a burial ground. It stood in open grassland on a slightly sloping spot. Burials took place as early as 3100

BC, when the first circular bank and ditch enclosure were being built around a simple monument for the burials. Burials continued for at least another five hundred years, when the giant stones that mark the landmark were put up. To honor the dead, the builders placed the bones of deer and oxen—as well as some worked flint tools—in the bottom of the ditch.

"Stonehenge, as a monument of stones, evolved in several construction phases spanning at least some fifteen hundred years. There is little or no direct evidence for the construction techniques used by the Stonehenge builders. However, conventional techniques using Neolithic technology have been demonstrably effective at moving and placing stones this size.

"More recently, two major new theories have been proposed that suggest Stonehenge was part of a ritual landscape and was joined to Durrington Walls by their corresponding avenues and the River Avon. The surrounding area was a land of the living, while Stonehenge was a domain of the dead. A journey along the Avon to reach Stonehenge was part of a ritual passage from life to death, to celebrate past ancestors. There is also evidence that Stonehenge was a place of healing. Trauma deformity in some of the graves may account for the high number of burials in the area.

"All the theories suggest that priests and astrologers over the years made rules and laws for the justification of where to put the stones. The same ideas apply to the wooden columns in Durrington Walls. The focus is on religious observance and the laws of their religion. They based their laws on many years of observing nature. Religions rest mostly on their dogma rather than the love of a supreme being. The concern is to occupy the people's attention. This replaces the true service of a supreme being and the concern for others.

"In the case of Stonehenge the priests and astrologers were too stuck on their own authority to allow people to be free and to function as mature people. This was their subtle form of abuse. All too soon, the stars shifted one degree over a hundred years. During their lifetimes, they didn't notice this small change. By the time they had the stones built, their calendar that predicted the solstices and equinoxes didn't match the movements of the sun, moon, and stars to the stationary stones. It was against their religion to change their calendar. Moving the stones and understanding why they had to be moved was an absurd possibility. Their religion and religious observances tried to adapt, but their thinking stayed in a box. We don't currently know what happened to the original people."

The boy *felt proud*.

"Well, that's the end of my story. It's my theory of how religions begin and in a way of how they become extinct like the dinosaurs. They can only exist for their moment in the arrow of time when they adapted to the changes in nature. If they do continue over the ages, they must adjust to the laws of science and integrate the logical truth of science with the intuitive values of their religion. I believe that neither science nor religion is static. The people must change when new evidence is available to justify a change. The religions can't be stereotyped. The people can't let their hypocrisy overcome them. They can't let their cynical character deny the goodness and love of their deepest human motives."

Dialogue Fifty-Three
The Star of Bethlehem[96]

"That's so right," said The Man. "Nevertheless, let us be sure we understand the stereotyping in our thinking and feelings. I want to clear up these ideas about religion and being religious. You also did a PowerPoint presentation about the Star of Bethlehem, didn't you?"

"Yes, we did. It's a favorite. We show it during the Christmas season in the planetarium."

"Look up the quote from Matthew about the star," the Man said.

"Okay, I have the quote of the Magi's visit in my computer. Yeah, here it is … Matthew 2:1–2. 'After Jesus had been born at Bethlehem in Judaea during the reign of King Herod, suddenly some wise men came to Jerusalem from the east, asking, 'where is the infant king of the Jews? We saw his star as it rose and have come to do him homage.'[97]

"My notes go on to say that the visit of the Magi took place at least several months after Jesus was born. Their visit is traditionally celebrated on Epiphany, January 6, in Western Christianity. My notes point to the fact of that that date is from a modern-day calendar. Many modern bible scholars think the author of the Gospel of Matthew created the story of the star.

"My personal opinion is that most bible scholars have trouble with calendars from different eras because of the difficulty with the concept of the arrow of time. It was hard to get a consistent time frame with all the different calendars in use at the time of Matthew's Gospel. Although the Julian calendar dominated in the past. I heard that modern scientists had a sixty-one second minute rather than a sixty second minute to start the new year of 2009. This adjusted their cesium clocks world wide."

He hesisted, then said, "We present in the planetarium that Christians generally regard the star as a miraculous sign given by God to mark the birth of Christ. Some theologians claimed that the star fulfilled a prophecy. In modern times, astronomers like those in the planetarium have proposed various explanations for the star. A nova which is an exploding star. A planet like Venus at its brightest. A comet with a long tail zooming across the sky. An eclipse of the Moon and

Jupiter or Saturn. And maybe a conjunction when the Moon, Jupiter, Saturn, and perhaps Venus are close together in the sky.

"These ideas have all been suggested. The star has also been interpreted as an astrological event. We can show each of these events on the planetarium dome and on screens positioned on the walls. But a big hero came along with a fantastic piece of research.

"Present-day astronomer and physicist Michael R. Molnar[98] has written a book using astronomical, astrological, and historical clues to solve the great mystery of the star. If I understand the modern process, one can program a computer to make an ephemeris from 10 BC to 0 BC in order to do horoscopes. An ephemeris is a day-to-day position of the sun, moon, and planets. As astrologers, the Magi learned how to make an ephemeris for the sun and moon and for the five planets: Mercury, Venus, Mars, Jupiter, and Saturn. They were able to make horoscopes and predict the future for the kings at the their time in history.

"The astrologers also created the zodiac. It served as the background for observing the movements of the sun, moon, and planets over many years. The ephemeris was the storehouse of all this information. The focus on making horoscopes gave the astrologers a profound edge in information. The astrologers' usefulness to the priests and kings helped the authorities with the religious observance and the laws of their religion. The people in charge of the religions favored the endless rules and customs, practices, rituals, and traditions because they increased their power. They structured people's lives with their power. The laws again replace the true service of a supreme being and the concern for others. Astrologers were important people at the time.

"The horoscopes at the time of the Magi started predicting a royal birth, likely to be in the period from 8 to 4 BC. During this time, the sun, moon, and planets moved majestically through the zodiac, forming fantastic aspects with each other. Only once, on April 17, 6 BC, would the sun, moon, planets, houses, the aspects between them, and all other special aspects be perfectly exact for the time of birth of a royal person. For sure, there would be perfection for a royal birth. This configuration could happen again maybe every fifteen hundred years or so. However, the best computers would never again predict the universe to line up with this majestic perfection as it did on April 17, 6 BC. This is what Michael R. Molnar found in his research. This was the birthday of Jesus Christ."

The boy looked at The Man, and a wry grin came upon his face. Each took his own forefinger and flicked his nose. This was their secret. The boy waited for a while before he continued reading from his computer screen.

"The big bang signifies the birth of the universe. Those two astronomical events plus my continual understanding of the moral laws are enough to convince me that love is Time. Would I be willing to accept anything less then the Trinity?

"The Roman Empire controlled the eastern Mediterranean. The body of people called the Christian Church lived under Roman laws. They quickly grew in size and influence over a few decades, and by the fourth century, they had become the dominant religion within the Roman Empire.

"The administrative model of the Romans became the administrative body of the Church. They lived by the Julian Calendar established by Julius Caesar in 46 BC. The stars still shifted one degree over a hundred years. However, the Church found ways to adapt to the seasons. Advent was forty days before Christmas, which was close to the shortest day of the winter solstice. The last full moon before the vernal equinox signified fourteen days before Ash Wednesday, which was the first day of Lent and forty days before Easter. Easter was always close to the vernal equinox. These patterns became the traditions and rituals of the Church. The religion and religious observances adapted just enough to keep their thinking in and out of the box. The authority of the Church grew over the years, and it became dogmatic in its teaching. It was very slow to change. The Church finally changed to the Gregorian calendar. January 11, 1732 became January 21, 1732. The people wanted their eleven days back."

The boy had simplified in his notes the dogma of the church. "To Christians, Jesus Christ is a teacher who reveals God. He is the incarnation of God. He is the savior and redeemer of humanity. He suffered, died, and was buried. His resurrection brought salvation from sin. He ascended into heaven, and most denominations teach that

Jesus will sit at the right hand of God to judge the living and the dead, granting everlasting life to his followers.

"So … you want to know the point?" asked the boy. The Man nodded.

"People tried to love 'unto others,' but the chain of command model of management over the years gave into rigid rules and laws that were torturous and abusive for the sake of power. "Stonehenge is the same scenario. The people build a monument to honor their dead. They put the stones into a configuration to worship the seasons, the sun, and the moon. They have two areas, one for life and one for death. They created traditions, practices, rituals, and rights. Their culture falls apart when their monument no longer serves its pupose.

"The Star of Bethlehem signified Your birth. The seeable Universe displayed itself majestically as a birthday present to You.

"The big bang signified the birth of the universe. Those two astronomical events were gifts from the Father to show His love.

"The Father created life to share in His Time. He gave us the free will to love Him in a face to face intimate relationship. Instead of a linear chain of command of control, I now realize that the Father thinks in terms of circles and spheres. We pass our love across and around with no conditions or strings attached. We continually share the understanding of the moral laws with the myriad of languages. All of this is enough to convince me that His love is His Time. Would I be willing to accept anything less then The Father, Son and Holy Spirit?"

Dialogue Fifty-Four
Altruism, Agape, Unconditional Love

The boy answered the question. "No! I don't think my heart, mind, or soul would ever be satisfied unless I communicate with you. I formed a bond with You, and I promised to keep my word."

The Man was getting excited about the next five Dialogues. He was standing with His left foot on the ground and His right foot planted firmly on the rock. His right leg bent at the knee and hip, with His right hand resting on His right thigh. He was reminiscing.

"Do you remember us talking about the year two thousand?" asked The Man, "That was when the first draft of the human genome, the DNA of the human species, was assembled."

"Yeah, I remember. Bill Clinton was the president, and Francis S. Collins was the scientist. Bill Clinton said, 'We are learning the language of life.' And Dr. Collins said, 'How humbling and awe-inspiring it was for him.'"

After a long pause, the boy continued. "I read his book, *The Genetic Language of God.*[99] You know Dr. Collins was head of the Human Genome Project. I have nothing but praise for him. I like what he said. He deserves a lot of credit for his words and language. I have paraphrased and copied the words from his book into my computer. In addition, I have also added my notes from my biology classes at college and high school. You can feel from his writings that he is a very humble person.

"I think it was Sir Isaac Newton who said that he stood on the shoulders of giants and saw grand vistas before him. I feel the same way about Dr. Collins; he saw grand vistas in DNA."

He told the boy to listen to his words:
In the modern era of cosmology, evolution and the human genome, with math as the tool of science, there must be a way to embrace both realms between the scientific and spiritual worldviews. [100]

"You know, I agree with his words and ideas, the boy said. "Can I read his words aloud to You?" The Man corrected. "May I?"

The boy was oblivious to the correction. "Sure, can I?"

The Man could only laugh. The nineteen-year-old boy was still a little boy in many ways.

The boy started reading his notes on Dr. Francis S. Collins from his computer:

Right and wrong is a clue to the meaning of the universe. Moral law is a universal feature of human existence. We feel from moral law the altruistic impulse, the voice of conscience calling us to help others. Altruism does not mean you scratch my back, I'll scratch yours. Altruism is more interesting: the truly selfless giving of oneself to others with absolutely no secondary motives. When we feel that kind of love and generosity, an awe and reverence overcomes us.[101]

The boy paused to let the words sink in, and then he continued:

Agape is different from friendship, affection, or romantic love. Their reciprocal benefit is easier to understand. Agape, or selfless altruism, presents a major challenge for the evolutionist. Agape cannot account for the drive of individual selfish genes wanting to perpetuate themselves. Quite the contrary, it may lead humans to make sacrifices that lead to great personal suffering, injury, or death, without any evidence of benefit.[102]

The boy had a puzzled look. "Are altruism and agape higher emotional states that can override our basic emotions of fear, doubt, pain, and guilt?" He looked to The Man for an answer. The Man sat quietly waiting for the boy to find an answer. When he didn't get one, the boy asked, "What about unconditional love?"

The Man could now give a whole answer, so He replied, "Yes, altruism, agape, and unconditional love are the highest emotional states a human being can experience!" The Man took over the discussion. He spoke Dr. Collins's words without notes.

If we are looking for benevolent coddling and indulgence, God is just a wish fulfillment. That's not what we find here. Instead, we come to grips with the existence of the moral law, as Dr. Collins calls it. With our obvious inability to live up to it, we realize that we are in deep trouble. We are potentially separated, eternally, from the author of that law. After all, we have free will, the ability to do as we please. We use this ability frequently to disobey the moral law.[103]

The Man continued to paraphrase Dr. Collins. Imitating Dr. Collins, he went on to inquire:

Why would a loving God allow suffering in the world? We answered this same question before. Dr. Collins goes on to his answer. What we do to one another brings about our suffering. It is humankind, not God, that has invented knives, arrows, guns, bombs, and all manners of other technologies of torture used through the ages. It is our intent to use science more for destruction rather than construction.[104]

The Man requested an answer from the boy. "Do you remember the bet we made about there being a God?"

"Yeah!" he replied. "About our conversation about God being a deist or a theist?"

"Of course."

The Man returned to the words of Dr. Collins:

The theist uses the moral laws to seek a God who not only set the universe in motion, but also takes an interest in human beings.[105]

Dialogue Fifty-Five
God, DNA, and RNA

The Man continued paraphrasing Dr. Collins's words:

A theist argues: If God exists, then He is supernatural. If He is supernatural, then He is not limited by natural laws. If He is not limited by natural laws, there is no reason He should be limited by the arrow of time. If He is not limited by the arrow of time, then He is in the past, the present, and the future.[106]

The boy interjected, "We used the idea of being in the now."

The Man returned to Dr. Collins:

The consequence of those conclusions would include four concepts. He could exist before the big bang. He could exist after the universe fades away, if it ever does. He could know the precise outcome of the formation of the universe even before it started.[107]

The boy interrupted loudly. "We used the words that God is Time! I disagree about knowing the precise outcome! What about knowing our ideas of the toy boat? What about knowing the math of chaos? This allows God to 'be in the now,' which we found out was different than past, present, and future."

The Man acted astonished. He had foreknowledge of the boy's behavior; therefore, He explained to the boy that it was like modeling a hurricane.

"Using chaos, you can predict the path of a hurricane within certain parameters. We can also predict your behavior within certain parameters; therefore, Dr. Collins is right if he allows his models certain parameters instead of precise outcomes." The Man continued. "Let's get back to Dr. Collins's words, and his fourth concept."

God could have foreknowledge of a planet near the outer rim of an average spiral galaxy that would have just the right characteristics to allow life. This would be Earth. He could have foreknowledge that the planet would lead to the development of sentient creatures, through the mechanism of evolution by natural selection. He could even know in advance the thoughts and actions of those creatures, even though they themselves have free will.[108]

The boy added, "Within certain parameters."

The Man added His own words: "God is not deterministic. He allows for determinism. He allows for chaos. To God, a satisfying harmony exists between science and belief."

The boy again offered his thoughts. "All laws are guides. Only the intolerant and blind obey them without question. The laws are like models. They can predict within certain parameters."

The Man responded again, using Dr. Collins's words to describe different systems of religion.

Harmony between science and belief is all-resonant with Buddhism, where an oscillation universe would be more compatible. The theistic branches of Hinduism encounter no major conflict with the big bang. Neither do most interpreters of Islam. Pope Pius XII was a strong supporter of the big bang theory even before its scientific underpinnings were well established.[109]

He continued using Dr. Collins's words:

The advances of science in the modern age have come at the cost of certain traditional reasons for belief in God.

The boy added his beatitude: "We mourn with happy tears this passing. The believer should not deny science. He should be embracing it." The boy added his knowledge of history. "Galileo is a perfect example of a scientist upsetting the traditions of the Catholic Church." The boy continued to espouse his knowledge. "The complexity of earthly life, implying the handiwork of an intelligent designer, is indeed reason for awe and for belief in God. If God is truly almighty, our puny efforts to understand the workings of His natural world will hardly threaten

Him. Science may answer its questions: 'How does life work? Why is there life anyway? Why am I here?'" The boy paused, wanting The Man to answer. He didn't respond. Therefore, the boy put his emphasis on Dr. Collins's words.

Presumably, almost four billion years ago, single-celled organisms were capable of information storage, probably using DNA, and were self-replicating and capable of evolving into multiple different types. We do not know how self-replicating organisms arose in the first place. How could a self-replicating information-carrying molecule assemble spontaneously from these compounds or similar compounds within meteorites?[110]

The boy was impressed with Dr. Collins's words, language, understanding, and wisdom. The more he learned, the more he was able to put into consciousness the path his life was following. He was beginning to understand his genetic gifts, and how they were adapting to his trials and tribulations of abuse. His compounds were evolving using his understanding of Dr. Collins's ideas.

These compounds are important biological building blocks, such as amino acids. DNA, with its phosphate-sugar backbone and intricately arranged organic bases, stacked neatly on top of one another and paired together at each rung of the twisted double helix, seems an utterly improbable molecule to have 'just happened,' especially since DNA seems to possess no intrinsic means of copying itself. RNA seems to be the potential first life form, since RNA can carry information, and in some instances, it can catalyze chemical reactions in ways that DNA cannot. DNA is something like the hard drive on a computer: it is supposed to be a stable medium in which to store information. RNA, by contrast, is more like a zip disk or a flash drive—it travels around with its programming and is capable of making things happen on its own.[111]

Dialogue Fifty-Six
The Words of Francis S. Collins

The boy continued to take charge. He liked studying biology in college. He liked giving Dr. Collins credit for his words. He told The Man, "I didn't copy Dr. Collins's book word for word on my computer. It was fun trying to add my words to his. So, I'll just be reading paraphrases regarding evolution and DNA."

Some critics often raise objections to any possibility of the spontaneous origin of life on Earth, based on the second law of thermodynamics. The second law states that in a closed system, where neither energy nor matter can enter or leave, the amount of disorder—more commonly known as 'entropy'—will tend to increase over time.[112]

Since life forms are highly ordered, some have argued that it would therefore be impossible for life to have come into being without a supernatural creator. But this betrays a misunderstanding of the full meaning of the second law: order can certainly increase in some part of the system, as happens every time you put away the dishes, but that will require an input of energy, and the total amount of disorder in the entire system cannot decrease. [113]

In the case of the origin of life, the closed system is essentially the whole universe, energy is available from the sun, and so the local increase in order that would be represented by the first random assembly of macromolecules, would in no way violate this law.[114]

Learning to understand the works of great men and women was so rewarding to the boy. He looked to The Man and said, "That's why I want to be a physicist. The three laws of thermodynamics are pretty heady stuff. I know the first law is conservation of energy. The second law is entropy. In addition, the third law is about available free energy, like the sun gives off. So I guess that there is energy available within certain parameters for DNA and RNA to do their job."

The Man was pleased with the boy's wondering, so there was no need to criticize his guessing. He redirected the boy's imagination back to the words of Dr. Collins. "Read some more," He directed.

Given the inability of science thus far to explain the profound question of life's origins, some theists have identified the appearance of RNA and DNA as a possible opportunity for divine creative action. If God's intention in creating the universe was to lead to creatures with whom He might have fellowship, namely human beings, and if the complexity required to start the process of life was beyond the ability of the universe's chemicals to self-assemble, couldn't God have stepped in to initiate the process? [115]

The boy looked at The Man for reassurance. He got a smile.

Darwin developed the theory of evolution by natural selection. He held that variation within a species occurs randomly, and that the survival or extinction of each organism depends upon its ability to adapt to the environment.

Mendel and Garrod added mathematical specificity to the notion of heritability in humans. DNA by James Watson and Francis Crick forms a double helix, a twisted ladder, and has information-carrying capacity that is determined by the series of chemical compounds that comprise the rungs of the ladder. [116]

The boy heard the excitement in The Man's voice as He interjected about the language that Dr. Collins discovered in the medium. He spoke eloquently about Dr. Collins's achievements of understanding the extraordinary qualities of the coding language of DNA.

The extraordinary qualities of DNA are brilliant in its solution to the problem of coding life's design. We should be in awe of this molecule. Its benefit is life. [117]

Its remarkable features include the outside backbone made up of a monotonous ribbon of phosphates and sugars. The rungs of the ladder are made up of combinations of four chemical components called bases. The chemical names of these DNA bases are A, C, G, and T. Each has a particular shape. The A shape fits neatly only on a ladder rung next to the T shape, and the G shape can fit only next to the C shape. These are 'base pairs.'[118]

Picture the DNA molecule as a twisting ladder, with each rung made up on one base pair. There are four possible rungs: A-T, T-A, C-G, and G-C. If any base is damaged, it can be easily repaired. One can think of DNA as an instructional script, a software program, sitting in the nucleus of the cell. Its coding language has only four letters in its alphabet.[119]

Hundreds or thousands of letters of code make up a particular instruction, known as a gene. All of the elaborate functions of the cell, even in as complex an organism as ourselves, have to be directed by the order of letters in this script.[120]

This program is run by messenger RNA. The DNA information that makes up a specific gene is copied into a single-stranded messenger RNA molecule, something like a half ladder with its rungs dangling from a single side. The half ladder moves from the nucleus of the cell, the information storehouse, to the cytoplasm, a highly complex gel mixture of proteins, lipids, and carbohydrates, where it enters an elegant protein factory called the ribosome. A team of sophisticated translators in the factory then read the bases protruding from the floating half ladder messenger RNA to convert the information in this molecule into a specific protein, made up of amino acids.[121]

Three rungs of RNA information make one amino acid. Proteins, amino acids, do the work of the cell and provide its structural integrity. The elegance of DNA, RNA, and protein continues to be a source of awe and wonder.[122]

The thrill is understanding the language of genetics.[123]

CHAPTER TEN
A nineteen-year-old boy learns about DNA & Chaos

Dialogue Fifty-Seven
God's Short Stories, Words, and Language Are Simple

The boy was astonished. The Man definitely had a propensity for words and language. The boy focused on The Man as he commenced to speak with his own words.

"The elegance of DNA, RNA, and protein continues to be a source of awe and wonder. What a fantastic language We created to describe each living species. This language is not just for human beings. There are sixty-four possible three-letter combinations of *A, C, T,* and *G,* but only twenty amino acids. This means a built in redundancy[124].

"We—the Father, the Son, and the Holy Spirit—created life that was so awesome in its scope, yet so simple in its letters and words. The combinations allow for infinite variations."

The Man explained further: "Each species is a poem in the offering. Each species is a scientific wonder. The scientist and the prophet poet with the language of metaphors—the arrow of time being a river; the tiger being the emotions and feelings; the fire being the ambitious aspirations of how the mind works—describe the indefinite variations of life on Earth."

The Man again became the verbal narrator. He had a predilection for Dr. Collins's words.

Investigations of many organisms, from bacteria to humans, revealed that this 'genetic code,' by which information in DNA and RNA is translated into protein, is universal in all known organisms. No Tower of Babel is allowed to confuse the language of life. The language of DNA is definite. GAG means glutamic acid in the language of soil bacteria, the mustard weed, the alligator, and your Aunt Gertrude.[125]

"Wait!" yelled the boy. "If I understand the Tower of Babel, it is the way God confused the one language of the builders and dispersed the people to all points of the earth. Therefore, what Dr. Collins is saying is that there is no confusion in the language of DNA. The one language of DNA is spread to all points of the earth. The combinations allow for indefinite variations.

"Wow! God is something! One language at the Tower of Babel dispersed into many languages all over the earth, because of pride. Yet God makes one language for all DNA that is dispersed worldwide as different species adapt and evolve."

The Man said, "You got it right. Dr. Collins goes on to explain how they learned to read the language." The Man switched to Dr. Collins's words:

Chemical wonders, including proteins that act like scissors or glue, have enabled scientists to manipulate DNA and RNA by stitching together bits and pieces of these instructional molecules from different sources. This collection of molecular biological laboratory tricks is recombinant DNA. To explain all these tricks are molecular mechanisms, genetic pathways, and natural selection.[126]

Many people who have considered all the scientific and spiritual evidence still see God's creative and guiding hand at work. The glorious beauty of a flower or the flight of an eagle could come about only as the consequence of a supernatural intelligence.[127]

Totally appreciated are complexity, diversity, and beauty. How marvelous and intricate life turns out to be! How deeply satisfying is the digital elegance of DNA! How aesthetically appealing and artistically sublime are the components of living things, from the ribosome that translates RNA into protein, to the metamorphosis of the caterpillar into the butterfly, to the fabulous plumage of the peacock attracting his mate!'[128]

Evolution as a mechanism can be and is true. However, that says nothing about the nature of its author. For those who believe in God, there are reasons now to be more in awe, not less.[129]

The boy was definitely in awe. Another of The Man's spellbinding orations had mesmerized him. How could he have ever felt rejection or anger toward this Man? He knew The Man wanted the truth of this whole business of DNA out in the open.

The Man's words crashed in his head as he remembered The Man's challenges: "I want you to start your hunger and thirst for righteousness with Me. I want you on the lookout; I want you in search of something great: like true justice, true good, or true reality."

The boy knew his destiny. This was justice. This was his beatitude to follow. He came out of his reverie. He picked up The Man's voice talking about Dr. Collins's accomplishments.

When we survey the vast expanse of the human genome, 3.1 billion letters of the DNA code arrayed across twenty-four chromosomes, several surprises are immediately apparent. There are only about twenty to twenty-five thousand protein-coding genes in the human genome. The total amount of DNA used by those genes to code for protein adds up to a measly 1.5 percent of the total.[130]

After a decade of expecting to find at least one hundred thousand genes, many of us were stunned to discover that God writes such short stories about humankind. His letters, words, and language are simple.[131]

The Man summarized for the boy. "This was shocking because gene counts for other simpler organisms such as worms, flies and simple plants seem to be in about the same range, namely around twenty thousand. A human's complexity must arise not from the number of separate instruction packets, but from the way they are organized. Perhaps our component parts have learned to multitask."

"Yeah!" yelled the boy. "KISS! Keep it simple, Spirit!"

Dialogue Fifty-Eight
The Rhetoric of The Man

The Man continued to paraphrase Dr. Collins:

Population geneticists, whose discipline involves the use of mathematical tools to reconstruct the history of populations of animals, plants, or bacteria, look at these facts about the human genome and conclude that they point to all members of our species having descended from a common set of founders, approximately ten thousand in number, who lived about 100,000 to 150,000 years ago. This fits well with the fossil record.[132]

"Man! This is some learning," the boy marveled.
The Man paid no attention to the boy. He was into his subject.

A tremendous surprise happened from genetic sleuthing. Two significant changes have occurred in the coding region of a language gene, apparently as recently as 100,000 years ago. A hypothesis suggested by collected data is that recent changes in a gene may have in some way contributed to the development of language in human beings.[133]

Godless materialists might be cheering, but it does not tell us what it means to be human. DNA sequence alone, even accompanied by a vast trove of data, will never explain certain special human attributes, such as the knowledge of natural laws, moral laws, and the universal search for God.[134]

"Oh, yeah," said the boy. "The laws are only guides. They are not absolute or perfect. The laws and the language of DNA don't tell us about the gravity of the sun and Earth. And vice versa: the mathematical language of gravity does not tell us about the origins of species." The boy went into deep thought. "I get it! Every system has its own set of laws. But I don't want to be a lawyer arguing law."

The Man tolerated the boy's interruptions. It was his freedom to learn. The Man picked up the thread of conversation and continued the theory of evolution according to Dr. Collins.

Darwin's framework of variation and natural selection is unquestionably correct. Perhaps part of the problem relates to a simple misunderstanding of the word 'theory.' Critics are fond of pointing out that evolution is 'only a theory.' Scientists are used to a different meaning of the word. Critics define theory as a speculative or conjectural view of something. Whereas scientists define theory as the fundamental principles and experiments underlying a system of science that proves that science describes reality with some truth. [135]

The boy had looked up Dr. Collins on the Internet. What an extraordinary combination: Dr. Collins had that rare gift of being a devout Christian as well as a great scientist. The boy returned to listening to The Man talk to him about St. Augustine and the YEC—Young Earth Creationists. [136]

"Saint Augustine [137] put down his thoughts about sixteen hundred years ago. In the first paragraph of 'Confessions,' he describes his longing for God: 'Nevertheless, to praise you is the desire of Man, a little piece of your creation. You stir man to take pleasure in praising you because you have made us for yourself, and our heart is restless until it rests in you.'

The Man continued, "Many YEC and other believers see scientific advances as threatening to God. However, does the Father really need defending?"

The boy answered. "I may be becoming a little prejudiced and opinionated, but I think The Father is the author of the laws of the universe. He is the greatest scientist, physicist, mathematician, and biologist. Most important, how can a person ignore rigorous scientific conclusions about His creation. Those who would demand that His people believe otherwise dishonor him.

The many forms of intellectual abuse entered the boy's mind. The three words that lead to abuse jumped at him: stereotype, prejudice, and bias. *Can faith in a loving God be built on a foundation of lies about nature and His mathematical laws of nature? But here is where my set of rules and values differ from the YEC. If I force my set of rules and values on them, then I am abusing them. If they force their rules and values on me, then I am the abused one.*

The Man was vehement against those who dishonored the Father. His voice resembled the strength of many as He spoke the next words: "The image of God as a cosmic trickster seems to be the ultimate admission of defeat for the creationist perspective. Would God, the Father, as the great deceiver, be an entity one would want to worship? Is this consistent with everything else we know about God from the Bible, from the moral law, and from every other source—namely that He is loving, logical, and consistent.

"As believers, you are right to hold fast to the concept of God as Creator. You are right to hold fast to the truths of the Bible. You are right to hold fast to the conclusion that science offers no answers to the most pressing questions of human existence. However, intelligent design—ID[138] portrays the Almighty as a clumsy Creator, having to intervene at regular intervals to fix the inadequacies of His own initial plan for generating the complexity of life. For a believer who stands in awe of the almost unimaginable intelligence and creative genius of God the Father, this is a most unsatisfactory image."

The Man was having so much fun with the words and ideas of Dr. Collins. He could use his voice, the words, and his knowledge of language in so many ways. His rhetoric was unbelievable. Using Dr. Francis Collins's rhetoric, The Man settled comfortably into a synthesis generally referred to as "Theistic Evolution."[139] He orated, as Dr. Collins, by stating, "Theistic Evolution is the dominant position of serious believers. It is the view espoused by many Hindus, Muslims, Jews, and Christians, including Pope John Paul II. There are many subtle variants of TE, but a typical version rests upon the following premises:

The universe came into being out of nothingness, approximately fourteen billion years ago. Despite massive improbabilities, the properties of the universe appear to have been precisely tuned for life. While the precise mechanism of the origin of life on Earth remains unknown, once life arose, the process of evolution and natural selection permitted the development of biological diversity and complexity over long periods of the arrow of time.

The Man finished His oration.

Dialogue Fifty-Nine
The Six Premises for the Creation

The genetic language of God discovered by Dr. Francis S. Collins enraptured The Man. Dr. Collins worked hard finding the words and language in the medium. The Man honored Dr. Collins by paraphrasing his words. There could be no greater praise. The Man was anxious to finish talking about Dr. Collins's ideas, however.

"Once evolution got under way, no special supernatural intervention was required. Humans are part of this process, sharing a common ancestor with the great apes. But humans are also unique in ways that defy evolutionary explanation and point to our spiritual nature. These include the existence of the moral law, the knowledge of right and wrong and the search for God that characterizes all human cultures throughout history.[140]

"If one accepts these six premises …"

The thought came to the boy that they would be the set of rules that would guide his thinking.

"… then an entirely plausible, intellectually satisfying, and logically consistent synthesis emerges: God, who is not limited in space or the arrow of time, created the universe and established natural laws that govern it.

1. God chose the elegant mechanism of evolution to create microbes, plants, and animals of all sorts.

2. He intentionally chose the same mechanism to give rise to special creatures that would have intelligence, knowledge of right and wrong, free will, and a desire to seek fellowship with him.

3. He had foreknowledge to know these creatures would ultimately choose to disobey the moral law.

4. This view is entirely compatible with everything that science teaches us about the natural world.

5. It is also entirely compatible with the great monotheistic religions of the world. Of course, the theistic evolution perspective cannot prove that God is real, as no logical argument can fully achieve that.

6. Belief in God will always require a leap of faith.[141]

The Man continued to heap his praise on Dr. Collins: "We aren't trying to wedge God into gaps in our understanding of the natural world; we are proposing God as the answer to questions science was never intended to address, such as 'How did the universe get here?' 'What is the meaning of life?' 'What happens to us after we die?'

"We are not creating a scientific theory. The heart, the mind, and the soul test the truth with spiritual logic. If God is outside of Nature, then He is outside of space and time. God is Time. In the moment of creation of the universe, God could have foreknowledge of the future. He could have details within certain parameters because he is not of the arrow of time. Evolution could appear to us to be driven by chance, but from God's perspective, the outcome would be entirely preordained.[142]

"Studies of human variation, together with the fossil record, all point to an origin of modern humans approximately one hundred thousand years ago. Genetic analyses suggest that approximately ten thousand ancestors gave rise to the entire population of six billion humans on the planet. We cannot believe that the Father, who created all the universe, and who communes with his people through prayer and spiritual insight, would expect people to deny the obvious truths of the natural world that science has revealed—or would expect people to deny reality in order to prove their love for him.

"The God of the Bible is also the God of the biological genome. He is worshiped in the laboratory as well as in the cathedral. His creation is majestic, awesome, intricate, and beautiful—and it cannot be at war with itself. Only we humans can start such battles. Only we can end them.[143]

"Even Albert Einstein[144] saw the poverty of a purely naturalistic worldview. Choosing his words carefully, he wrote, 'Science without religion is lame, religion without science is blind.'"

Dialogue Sixty
A Summary of the Ideas the boy Has Learned

They were in their garden. The Man was sitting on the rock. The boy was kneeling at his side and leaning on The Man. The sun's rays filtering through seemed more intense than usual. The Man looked intently at the boy with unconditional love. He spoke softly and gently to the boy.

"Well, my little big man, what have you learned? The Wisdom of Solomon? The righteousness of justice? The unconditional, altruistic, and agape form of love? The value of enlightenment that builds self-esteem … and self-respect that overcomes abuse?" The Man paused.

"Have you learned how to listen with your heart, mind, and soul? Have you learned the understanding of moral and natural laws?"

They remained silent for a long time. The nineteen-year-old boy no longer felt intellectually abused. He was deep in thought, contemplating his answers.

The Man gave him a hint. "Start backward and try to remember as much as you can about the ideas we covered." Silence permeated the garden under the trees.

"I remember …" The boy paused. Finally, he rattled off his answers. "I worked hard studying *The Language of God*, by Francis S. Collins, who is head of the Human Genome Project. 'Religion and hypocrisy so often go hand in hand. People claim to be one thing, but in their hearts and actions, they are the exact opposite.'

"A main theme for humans is to have an intimate relationship with God. God wants to connect with us. God has told us that the greatest gift of all—1 Corinthians 13:13[145]—is the emotion of love. However, other emotions are essential for our growth: fear, doubt, guilt, pain, and hundreds more. God wants us to connect with him through our feelings and emotions; we listen with our hearts, souls, and minds as he talks back to us.

"St. Paul's words were about the law. All who depend on the law are under a curse. No one is justified in God's sight by the law, for the just man shall live by faith. The law's terms are, whoever does these things shall live by them. If you break a law, you have sinned.

"I learned from Paul that moral and natural laws are guides. You must obey the laws, but not be a slave to them. You must be who you are, and not be obsessed with the laws, whether they be natural or moral.

"God wins the battle when we are conscious of our emotions of fear, doubt, pain, guilt, and love, and our sense of right and wrong makes a clear intelligent decision. 'Our river flows in peace. Our tiger preserves its forest. Our fire is used to anneal the mind.'

"You, my big Man, told me that You had doubts when praying in the Garden of Gethsemane. You felt the hypocrisy of the guilt from those who convicted You of a crime. You felt the fear of the impending evil of the cross. You endured the pain of the scourging and the nails. Out of love, You forgave those, for they did not know."

The boy continued, "I was so confused when you first gave me that order: 'I order you to memorize this statement. Are you ready? The master who believes he understands his slaves because they obey his orders would be intolerant and blind. Now I insist that you rescind that order.' I now understand that ordering, controlling, dictating, and being power hungry makes a person intolerant and blind. God is *not* intolerant or blind. He leads with love."

Dialogue Sixty-One
Chaos Theory[146]

Trying to be mysterious, with his fingers spread over his eyes like a mask, the boy spoke in an eerie tone.

I am Chaos; I am extremely sensitive to initial conditions. If you change the initial state of my system by a tiny amount, you change my future significantly. I am a new science, and you can call me by my name: chaos theory.[147]

"Scientists see me as a universal theory. I not only apply to physical problems, but also to problems in almost every topic worth studying. Ha-ha-ha! An extensive alphabetical list of my conquests is quite imposing: astronomy, biology, black holes, business, chemistry, colliding galaxies, economics, engineering, mathematics, medicine, physics, pulsating stars, and much more. Ha-ha!"

The boy was having so much fun. He was trying to put himself into the role of the dark infinity of space. He was trying to be the formless medium that preceded the existence of the ordered universe before the big bang. He continued speaking in his spooky way.

"Scientifically, I, as Chaos Theory, am more than random behavior, lack of control, or complete disorder. I can be deterministic.[148]

"Ah-ha! You know, I do have some scruples. Laws govern me. The laws give me mathematical structure and order. Why, I rank side by side as one of the most important discoveries of the twentieth century. Quantum theory, the theory of relativity, and the biological genome do not outclass my murky shadow.

"Oh, by the way, ole chaos here is not restricted to complex systems. I can lower myself to work on a simple system. Let it be known that many simple systems can behave chaotically." The boy raised his eyebrows. He gave a wicked smile that lit his eyes.

You do know that it is I, Chaos Theory, who best describes the formation of the universe. I can give solutions, in considerable detail, to problems between two interacting bodies in motion. Three interacting bodies, called three-body problems, are extremely difficult problems to solve.[149]*Have no fear! I, Chaos, am here, bringing these phantom problems to their solution. Ah, maybe!*

"The old deterministic approach worked well for simple systems but failed when applied to complex systems. The deterministic method appeared to fail when applied to a system of more than two interacting objects.

"Statistical approach, however, worked well when applied to complex systems. That is when I open the squeaky door to my private inner sanctum. I see in the dark shadows that the forces balance. Ah-ha! I know the system is stable.

"When I see with my super-duper ultra vision a slight change, an alien unbalanced force, I know this creates a large change in the future of the system; the state is unstable.[150]

"Do you want to know? Of course, you want to know if the solar system is unstable. Weak forces, say, those between the planets, could eventually cause the entire system to change dramatically. Ha-ha-ha!

"Have no fear! I, Chaos, am here, bringing the impending danger to the forefront. The evil, weak force will be seen for what it is.

"In nature, things aren't as cut-and-dried as they are in mathematics, but there is reasonably good agreement. Scientists have discovered through me, Chaos, that the solar system is not a precise machine. They now realize that through me, they live in a system beset with more complexity than they imagined.[151]" He continued portraying Chaos:

I, Chaos, have given them a much clearer picture of what is going on.

I, Chaos, am the frame that puts the picture into perspective. For example: The problem with general relativity is the equation itself. It is so complex that the most general solution has never been obtained. There is hope, for the equation has solved many simple systems.[152]

I, Chaos, am breaking through the thickheadedness of humans. I come from two major recent developments:

Breathtaking computing power enables researchers to perform hundreds of millions of complicated calculations in a matter of seconds, e.g., forecasting random changes in weather, hurricanes, tornados, and the spread of epidemics.

The rise in computing power accompanies a growing scientific interest in irregular phenomena: the metabolism of cells; the changing populations of insects and birds; the rise and fall of civilizations; the propagation of impulses along our nerves.[153]

I, Chaos, was born when these developments combined with the emergence of a new style of geometrical mathematics: beyond Euclid to non-Euclidean structures of fractal geometry.

I, Chaos, connect our everyday experiences to the laws of nature by revealing the subtle relationships between simplicity and complexity, and between orderliness and randomness.

I, Chaos, present a universe that is at once deterministic and obeys the fundamental physical laws, but the universe is also capable of disorder, complexity, and unpredictability.[154]

I, Chaos, cast doubt on the traditional model-building procedures of science.

I, Chaos, am strikingly beautiful in my entire enigmatic splendor.

The boy waved and wiggled his fingers in front of his face, trying to create mysteriousness. He proceeded to the next idea, trying to be even more dramatic.

"For example, there is the traditional model-building procedure of science that can lead to a discriminatory use of genetic information. It is the intent of the people using the method of science for their own personal benefit that can cause problems.

"Debating the morality from vastly different cultural backgrounds and religious traditions in a secular and pluralistic society is idealistic.

People use words from their culture that are ambiguous to people of other cultures. This makes it difficult to communicate. In a colloquial sense, people live on opposite side of the tracks and find it difficult to cross over. This happens under a moral set of laws where one's religion is the guide. One's religion in this case comes from a narrow range of principles and values.

"A particular set of genes dealt to a species reveals their gifts, traits, and who they really are. However, how they evolve is up to the species. Picking a change in the DNA sequence for selfish reasons is a violation of justice. It is making a species something other than it was meant to be. Predispositions, predetermination, genetic determinism, spiritual genetics, and the God gene are all initial conditions of DNA. Changing the initial conditions may lead to wide variations in the future."[155]

The boy crouched slowly into a bat-like figure, pulling a murky black silk cape around his body as he reclined on the mulch. He again spoke as Chaos:

I, Chaos, have my dark side. Hey, I feel no guilt. When humans use me, they cause the fear, doubt, and pain! The vicious, violent, evil aspects of torture, abuse, and crucifixion have a human's egotistical, warped, prideful mind to blame. Shame! Shame on you!

I, Chaos, can see the sciences of psychology using my vast cache of mathematical knowledge to study behaviors. Again, the question becomes, how do humans use me?

I, Chaos, can see the violations of justice and fairness in genetic manipulation. Flaws in DNA are essentially universal. No one gets to pick his own DNA sequence. Bio-ethical issues are complicated.

I am Chaos; I am extremely sensitive to initial conditions. If you change the initial state of the system by a tiny amount, you change its future significantly.

The boy slowly uncoiled as he stood. He removed his mask of fingers and slithered the cape to the floor. He bowed to his audience.

The Man applauded with one hand. Thus began the riddle of the one-handed applause.

CHAPTER ELEVEN
A boy learns about the riddle of God.

He becomes a man

Dialogue Sixty-Two
The Riddle[156]

"Well, little Man, I applauded you with one hand! Can you solve that riddle for me?"

The boy went into deep thought. Was The Man tricking him again? *Nah!* he thought. *The Man was open and honest and said it was a riddle. The Man must want me to use logic and think.*

Let's see, he kept thinking within himself. *I got a knuckle bump for summarizing. I got one-handed applause for acting out the chaos. Therefore, I have to do more than these two things.*

The boy knew he was good at asking questions, so that must be his first clue in solving the riddle. *So, what are the questions? That's dumb, asking a question to get questions.*

He wondered anyway and thought about three questions.

When would The Man applaud me? I don't know!

The answer will come from listening with my heart, mind, and soul. That's it! Just be quiet and listen.

Why would He applaud me?

I think the answer will come when I solve the riddle.

What do I have to do?

I must fulfill all the gifts He has given me.

Yes! he thought. *That's the answer!*

The boy remembered how he'd let the word altruism sink in. This was the voice of his conscience, a calling from God for him to help others. This was the feeling he got from understanding the moral and natural laws. This was his gift.

Altruism is the truly selfless giving of oneself to others with absolutely no secondary motives. When we feel that kind of love and generosity, an awe and reverence overcomes us. This is one of the greatest gifts.

The boy kept reflecting on the thoughts that were coming into his consciousness.

Agape is another gift. The Man told me it is the reciprocal benefit from friendship, affection, and romantic love. These are easier gifts to understand. Agape is the greater gift by means of the combining of lesser gifts.

Agape, or selfless altruism, may lead humans to make sacrifices that lead to great personal suffering, injury, or death, without any evidence of gaining a benefit.

Altruism, agape, and unconditional love are the higher emotional states of humans. The basic emotions of fear, doubt, pain, and guilt, along with others, are our everyday feelings. Our virtues and vices are our everyday actions and behaviors. Our value systems flow from all these emotions, feelings, and actions. These evaluate our experiences.

The boy felt good about his understanding of emotions.

We receive these gifts, along with our intellect, to decide, to choose, to do God's Will. This is the freedom given to us. The Crucifixion of The Man was His ultimate choice. The boy was thinking about his beatitudes when The Man broke into his thoughts.

The Man followed the boy's thoughts within certain parameters. However, He wanted the boy to voice aloud his thoughts about the riddle. Therefore, He spoke to the boy from a mind-set that 'our word is our bond.' Bonded to the boy by word is what he wished for.

"Think of what you have to do! When fear, doubt, guilt, and pain are the whirlpools in your life, that will be Me speaking to you. I'll accept your word when you call. We promised to love. You know there is chaos, and you know we can solve the problems. If you fail to call, then I'll know you have lost your word and your love. However, I'll still give you another chance. I'll find another way for you, for you were created to love.

"Although when you do love, anger may be a 'just' action. Like the behavior I had toward the moneychangers. It is almost impossible not to use all your emotions. Denying them will only lead to blind intolerance. God created you for intimacy by allowing you to use your emotions. All things touch something deep within you. God speaks to your heart. When unconditional love is first, and the greatest gift, all other emotions are viable. Elated emotions from achievements are only part of the riddle.

"You know that abuse and the rationality of the intellect disrupt our communication. Once math and science became dominant languages, it was almost impossible to form a bond. Our existence became questionable. We love you so much that we speak to you heart and soul and mind through your emotions. We don't have to prove our existence. You have your free will; however, we will always find a way to show you Our love.

The Man became quiet. The boy filled the silence.

"I remember when I would exaggerate all the time. My imagination was always running wild."

The boy added, "I remember when we talked about our listening being garbled. We said we don't pay attention and listen to people. We don't really care what they are saying. We just wait for a pause, so we can jump in with our own thoughts and biases and brag about our achievements."

The Man added, "People are like that to God. They can hear him a little, but they cannot make out much of what He is saying because they are more concerned with their own thoughts and achievements."

Dialogue Sixty-Three
Unconditional Love Is Equivalent to the Super Force[157]

They started to jog. When they reached the edge of the garden, they looked to the west to see the most beautiful red-orange sunset painted on the underside of the clouds.

"I know what makes the colors of the sunset," the boy said. "It's the size of the molecules in the sky that scatter the wave lengths of the light. The long waves of reds and oranges scatter off the big molecules in the clouds. The short waves of blues scatter off the small molecules of air."

The Man looked at the boy, marveling at what he saw. He was content with the thoughts of the boy. He would add other dimensions. He wanted the boy to feel what he experienced. He wanted the boy to add value to what he saw. He wanted the boy to be able to express his thoughts from both the heart and the mind.

In addition, the arrow of time was equal in importance to the other three dimensions of the boy's space. He wanted the boy to experience the arrow of time, to allow the reality of time to be totally experienced as the truth. He spoke to the boy.

"When you see science for what it is, it's scary in what it does. It is pragmatic yet mystical. It describes the universe as being so big in comparison to how small we are. The beauty of the universe— a rainbow, a sunset, a full moon rising—and all that is in it is awesome.

"The determinism, the rationalism, the intellectualism, and the high level of mathematics necessary to describe the forces of the universe do not detract from its beauty. Nevertheless, unconditional love is an equivalent force, part of the singularity, being a single source of love, if not greater than the super force of the big bang; it is an energy transfer between humans comparable to the four forces coming from the super force. The forces come from the loving essence of the Father. Abuse and crucifixion are opposite to love.

"Love is not described mathematically. Some people playacting as God describe love as Cupid, Eros, Aphrodite, Venus, and others. It is also described as people and cities: prostitutes and red light districts." The Man persisted with the many images of love and sex.

"Love is described as emotions leading to behaviors: ardor, passion, erotic, amorous, romantic, sex, sexual desire, lust, erogenous, carnal, venereal, an aphrodisiac, and others. Many words elicit the sought-after feelings of love. However, what is the true feeling of unconditional love?

"Are people just resigned to living with all these descriptions? Recovering what humanity lost is a slow person-by-person process. The human heart, once distanced from God, is not easily won back to its source of life and goodness. The Father is stern, but not intolerant or blind. He only asks for love.

"What is He? It doesn't seem fair, does it? Is He the deterministic deist? Alternatively, is He the rejected theist that felt the incredible feelings on the cross? I suffered the abuse and torture of the cross because of the laws for justice. This was the punishment for humanity's sins. Redemption was the payback for the sins written in the laws. The Mosaic Law steered the people through eddies of life to attain self-respect and self-esteem. The people couldn't care less because of the misuse of power and abuse. The Crucifixion was an evil, ugly achievement for the people at the time. The Resurrection was a glorious achievement of the Father.

"I became the captain of the ship," said The Man. "I was the pilot at the tiller. We made it through the whirlpools and back to the calm waters of the Father's loving forgiveness. Love goes beyond the moral and natural laws.

"What did you think of My metaphors?" asked The Man.

"Awesome ... all fired up!" replied the boy. "The Crucifixion is hate. The Resurrection is love."

"What we need to do now is to help you and a girl join in a relationship. As your Father, I am going to give you the advice of a lifetime. You have enough words to communicate, so listen carefully. Be careful of your pride that you don't brag. You just have to be yourself, have confidence. Learn to listen to her first, and then let the girl know who you are. You have enough love to share, so share it. Use it to get to know her. Learn to please her with things that she likes. Build her confidence, her self-esteem, and self-respect. Try to understand how she thinks and feels. Be sensitive to her emotions. Learn to read her nonverbal communication. True relationships help people grow and achieve their gifts. Give her lots of 'unto others.'

"This is what the Father does, and He wants the same for you. He helps you to listen and turn off your internal dialogue. You need his help, just as you need strong relationships with others. With hard work, practice, and perseverance you can hear, see, and feel another's communication. This brings us back to the idea of religion."

The boy had learned to notice the body language of The Man. It was not that He was frowning or scowling; His overall demeanor simply gave the impression that the idea of religion was not The Man's favorite subject. "You seem to still dislike religion. I thought we solved that problem with our understanding of Stonehenge and the Star of Bethlehem. I guess I'm still naïve."

The Man snapped back. "You know the difference between the two." There was a sharp ring to His voice as he continued. "Religion is not the same thing at all as being religious. They are opposites. Religion is an ideal. People practice their chosen religion to attain the values of the ideal. A theology develops to relate their quest to an environing culture. The theology becomes another set of laws, the rules of the religion. The intuitive rules of the religion become a compulsion, a habitual obsession.

"You know about the traditions, the rituals. Abiding by the rules is an outward show of achievement. The mantra is letting certain feelings show or not show!" The Man's voice lost the sharp ring. His whole demeanor softened. Something resplendent seemed to emanate from His being.

"We formed our bond. Our words are true. You strive for wisdom as your ultimate value. You discovered your beatitudes. You sought justice. You understood your gifts and had faith in them! You had love for yourself. You gave your love to others, no matter what differences or similarities you had. You were a new spirit, all fired up. In a way, this was your religion. However, you do not misuse power. You do not force others to have the same laws as you. You change. You grow. You evolve into the best you can be. Being religious is displaying the real you to others. You form a bond with all, and you keep your bond with the Father and Me."

Dialogue Sixty-Four
Love Is in Your Heart[158]

They continued jogging. It was getting dark, and the first and brightest stars came out. "Aren't they just beautiful," The Man said. "We can see, with the unaided eye, seven or eight magnitudes of stars. With a telescope and technological attachments, we can see an almost uncountable number of stars in their galaxies. The variety is almost limitless. What grandeur, what magnificence, and what glory … I could go on forever praising the Father for the creation. Oh, how We love it.

"Let us continue to speak about love. It is more than the right time to discuss love. You, my little big man, are neither too young nor would you ever be too old to learn about love. The Father is at all stages of love, whether it be the stages of altruism, agape, or unconditional love; or the stage of playacting by creating love goddesses similar to Cupid or Venus; or the stage of the actions between two consenting people. That is, people who want to connect with each other at a deep level. Love is always beautiful no matter what stage. It is the greatest emotional experience for humans.

"When a person misuses the word or emotion of love to indulge in his or her carnal desires by powerfully subjecting another person to defilement or debasement of his self, then this power causes grief, shame, and humiliation. This is abuse. No laws or rules could alter this kind of evil, ugly, or debasing behavior. The Bible tried to specify the laws, thus restricting the emotion of love. However, the people did not obey the laws. They misconstrued their emotions.

"The Bible is much more than a rulebook of laws. It is much more than how to be a good person. It is a story of love. Let us use the words and emotions to portray love in all its beautiful ways. Therefore, I, as The Man, with My masculine side, am going to allure you, a feminine side, My beloved, My soul mate. I will lead you into the desert and speak tenderly to you. I have engraved you on the palms of My hands. As the bridegroom rejoices over his bride, so I rejoice over you. Therefore, My heart yearns for you. One day, you will call Me 'my husband'; I will betroth you to Me forever; I will betroth you to Me in love. I have made Myself one spirit with you. I nourish you; I cherish you. I give Myself up for you. I lay down My life for you. The Father wants Me to say these words to you.

"Consequently, I have My softer side, My feminine side, the side that rocked you in the cradle, hugs you tight, and kisses you goodnight. I fed you. I nourished you. I bathed you. I clothed you. I was always there at your side when you called. I steadied you with your first steps. I helped you to speak your first words. I helped clear the road of obstacles. I watched you to grow.

"The Father wants to say words to you. Be silent in your mind; listen with your heart as He whispers your name. He wants to write your name on the palm of his hand as a symbol of his love for you. He is your altruistic lover. The Father comes through to you when you listen attentively. You do not need to talk. He wants you to fall in love when you read His Word. He wants to do these things, and so much more, to your heart.

"I listen to My Father's voice through My heart. Our hearts as humans change by deeply knowing the Father's heart toward us. He will find a way to share His love with you. He will forgive you until your free will rejects Him fully.

"Find a place like the garden. It is your special place to listen. In the midst of doubt, fear, guilt, pain and other emotions, the Father speaks to us. We are more prone to listen when we are in our special place. We are designed to be joined to the Father—to know his love, to relate to him intimately.

"We cannot ask the Father to overcome the world's evil and ugliness or evil and ugly behavior. There are no words to describe the nonsense of evil adequately. The Father gave us a fundamental nature in our DNA. Our intellect, our senses, our feelings, and our emotions are the essence of our nature. There are no reasons to manipulate our DNA or take away our senses, feelings, and emotions. They, along with an enlightened intellect, are our guides.

"Have faith! Believe in the Father. It breaks the Father's heart to see people suffer. However, our bond is in an altruistic, agape, unconditional love relationship with Him. One day the evil will be gone. Each will account for evil, abusive behaviors. Do you hear the words? They will solve the riddle."

Dialogue Sixty-Five
The Man, Father, Friend, Teacher[159]

"Do you now know what to do to solve the riddle?" There was a long pause, and the boy was mute. "I know you are still a young man, soon to be married. However, let us entertain ourselves with these questions: What kind of a dad do you think you will be? Why would I applaud you?" The Man paused. He started again by inundating the boy with more questions.

"Are you going to follow your real dad in ugly behavior? On the other hand, are you going to break the mold that abused children become abusing adults? Are you going to be a dad like the one you claim? For here are some of your claims. "I will reach for the Wisdom of Solomon. I will listen with my heart, soul, and mind for the altruistic, agape, unconditional love as the best model about being a dad.

"Moms can listen too! They can be in the same situation," the boy softly added.

The Man could feel a big grin spread over his face. A joy washed over him just thinking about the goals of the boy. The Man spoke to the boy with solemnity. His words were light. They were not a burden.

"If I give you some more hints of what you have to do to solve the riddle, will you promise me you will work your hardest to display these behaviors?"

The boy's pride was tweaked for a just a second. Then he realized The Man was his father, his teacher, and his friend. He nodded his head yes. His soft utterance of the word yes was the most humble word he had ever spoken.

The Man then started his list of hints. "When you hold your babies in your arms and look at them for the first time, you will feel love deeply in your heart and soul. These are the words of the Father speaking through Me. This is how he feels toward Me. In fact, you will hear His words coming through Me. However, they are coming from the Father as an introduction to you, my little big man. This is how He feels about you.

"Listen with your heart. Let your emotions well over. Let every emotion you possess fill you to the brim and overflow. Giving you these hints is how the Father and I feel toward you." He paused, making sure the boy was on task with the hints. "Your understanding of the arrow of time informs you of the precious little time you have to spend with a growing child. The times you feed them, the times you change their diapers, the times you bathe them, the times they are sleeping, the worry over the soft spot on the tops of their heads, the times they ride the pony on your swinging leg … There will be time for you to exercise them. It will be fun for you to sing to them all the psalms, fables, rhymes, and dumb little stories.

"You will remember your child's unique smell for a lifetime. Your child has the softness that will grow to show God's light. The child will have the DNA of you and your wife and the breath of the Holy Spirit. They mimic you in so many ways, with a combination of special touches. The beautiful child is there to reflect God's love. Do you now understand that when we capitalize Time, we make Time a name for the Father? You are Time to your child. The Father is Time to you. You are love.

"You delight in the happiness their achievements and curiosity bring them, even if it is fleeting. You help them find their gifts. You pay attention to their attitudes and temperament. You will make them try everything once, but never with a misuse of power. Baseball, football, basketball, swimming, ballet, gymnastics, track, pool, live Shakespeare on stage, and anything else that will fit the initial trial. There will be no quitting until they have had the experience. You delight in them and love their accomplishments. You wipe the tears from their eyes when they falter. The sound of their cries unties the strings to our hearts.

"They do not always obey. You learn to be tolerant, with an open mind and heart to their disobedience. You will try not to be mean or angry when you feel that they should be disciplined. You will try not to be mean or project your anger on them when it is you that is being self-centered and selfish."

Dialogue Sixty-Six
God Is Pleasure[160]

The boy was awestruck by The Man's words. The rhetoric painted a magnificent mosaic of values, language, experiences, and the arrow of time. Learning from The Man was an unbelievable pleasure. The Man would be his best friend forever. All he had to do was listen as The Man spoke to him, as He was doing now.

"As your children grow, you learn not to expect performances beyond their gifts. Their self-esteem and self-worth become the most cherished traits they can possess. You watch them perform through all their growing years. Sometimes your pride overcomes your common sense, and you push too hard. You marvel at how resilient and adaptable your children are to your mistakes.

"Don't you think it's possible that The Father would feel the same way about you that you feel about your kids? He loves you so much. He wants to give you the world. He wants to be as connected to you as you are to your children. He wants you as His child.

"If The Father designed people for an intimate connection with Himself, then we are incomplete without Him. The Father wants to love us with a passionate love. God is pursuing you. He wants you connected with Him forever. Don't you feel loved by God, much less pursued by Him? I am pursuing you, my little man. Do you know now what you are to do to solve the riddle?

"Yes, I am to love to achieve, and have faith that He loves. I am to become a reflection of the looking glass of Time. The Father is Time. His unconditional love is for all 'time.'"

The boy could not keep himself from asking a question. He finally learned to ask questions because he truly wanted to know the answer. "But what is pleasure from God?"

The Man answered him. "What if you could talk to the one who created the medium? The one who created words, language, and laws and made all knowledge available. The one who stirred the medium and created the big bang. The one who created the solar system. The one who created the Star of Bethlehem for the birthday of His Son. The one who sent the Holy Spirit with the gifts, the fruits, and the virtuous acts. The one who created the wonders of the world. The one who created the DNA molecule, which allows a heart, mind, and soul to exist. These are great achievements. You could talk about His achievements for the everlasting arrow of time. Your faith is for Time.

"His achievements may be fleeting, changing and evolving; nevertheless, His love is forever. God, without a doubt, is pleasure and fulfillment.

"We bond with you. We started this relationship of Dialogues with you. We covered your abuse, violence, crassness … and bet on you. We gambled that you would get through the eddies and whirlpools. We were betting on a sure thing that you would pass the tests, trials, and tribulations. We helped you to overcome by praise and love. Your achievements helped you to love.

"We are reaching out to you. That is why I became a person. We want to reach out to everyone. We will help everyone fulfill his or her gifts, fruits, and virtuous acts. Have Faith. However, self-centered ego gratification in achievements is hindering. You do not really need Me to show up. Letting go is the key to your achievements. We will applaud you with two hands when you change and become like a little child. You are of the greatest importance in the Kingdom of God when you believe having faith as a child is your top priority. Your self-centered learning deserved a one-handed applause for your performance of understanding the chaos theory and all that it encompasses. The hard work—learning science, math, languages, and seeking wisdom—satisfied your childlike curiosity. This was the one-handed applause for your achievements.

"The other hand was learning to overcome the traumas of abuse. You dealt with your emotions, your feelings, your values, your virtues, and your vices. This hand was your ability to learn to have faith in Me, and put into practice the three *omni* words and one *bene* word. You believed in the Father. You had faith in Me."

Dialogue Sixty-Seven
Epilogue

The boy, now a young man going on twenty, walked away from the tree-shaded garden, where the light flickered, filtering through the leaves. The young man knew he could come back anytime he pleased. This was his sanctuary. However, this was not his real world.

He would never forget being a young, wretched boy wailing away. He was writhing on the soft, mulchy ground in a rigid fetal position. His arms were wrapped around his bent-up knees with his head in his hands between his knees. His tears, mixed with blood, drenched the mulch from his cupped hands.

He appeared beaten, battered, and swollen, with black and blue marks over his body. He was stiffly rocking back and forth, retching the blood, tears, and spit from his nose and mouth. A few deep cuts in his brows and a huge gash on his cheek under his left eye required stitches. The cuts contributed to the ugliness of the violence he faced. He did not care if he lived or died. He rubbed the scars.

He remembered that The Man touched him. Even though he cowered at the touch, he felt the warmth spread through his body. He remembered expecting a kick. He thought of submitting himself to the inevitable. He had lost his desire to fight back. He was thinking about committing suicide.

He heard The Man humming in a soft, low baritone voice, barely loud enough to hear. Through his gloominess, he felt the song as clearly as heard the words. It had been a long time since anyone sang a lullaby to him. This kind of feeling was a new experience for him at that time.

He heard words in his thoughts from Matthew 11:28–30[161]: *Come to Me, all you who labor and are overburdened, and I will give you rest. Shoulder my yoke and learn from me, for I am gentle and humble of heart, and you will find rest for your souls. Yes, my yoke is easy, and My burden is light.*

The boy remembered feeling in his heart a different poetic lyric, with a weird language he'd never heard or felt before. He felt his heart was listening to a love song. His anguish was being soothed. He'd never felt anything like it before.

The Man sang the poetic lyric repeatedly. Each was more soothing than the last. The boy tried to open his eyes to see who was humming. One of his eyes was swollen shut. The other eye saw a blurry figure wrapped in smoke. The blurry figure looked strange. His clothes were clean but out of style. It was uncanny to the boy that He cast a simply dazzling aura.

With difficulty, the boy attempted to sit up. He came up with enough oomph to act out. From that moment, he started learning how to overcome his abuse by learning self-respect and gaining self-esteem with well-established values—and by learning about all that was in the creation. His top priority was believing in The Man and having faith in the Father, Son, and Holy Spirit.

As the young man reached the path out of the garden, he was reminiscing on what he'd learned from The Man. He took into account everything that was in the medium, on the Father's hard drive.

He envisioned the natural laws. They were the result of big bang. The super force split into the four main forces, forming the universe. The electromagnetic force, with the positive and negative charges of electricity, united with the attracting and repelling poles of a magnet. The strong and weak forces were the consequences of opposite forces of attraction and repulsion inside the nucleus of an atom. Einstein described the gravitational force as the curvature of space causing matter to move, and matter causing the space to curve. Each force had its own mathematical language describing it. The singularity of love was different. The Star of Bethlehem was the unconditional love of the Father.

He pictured the moral laws because of the beginning of language in human beings. Once let loose, the super force could not go back into a stable medium. The greatest commandment of all, written in two parts in all four gospels of the Bible, is the foundation of the moral laws.

The first is this: "The Lord our God is the one and only Lord, and you must love the Lord your God with all your heart, with all your soul, with all your mind, and with all your strength."

The second is this: "You must love your neighbor as yourself. There are no greater commandments than these. This commandment can be measured in 'unto others.'"

He turned his head to look back at the garden. He remembered the story of the two monks. He would no longer carry the weight of the abuse with him. He need not fear the past. He left the past in the garden. He would carry the light burden of its memory with him. The memory also included the forgiveness given to his mother and father. In his heart, he would unconditionally love them. The Man had taught him well. The young man believed in The Man.

Who is of the greatest importance in the Kingdom of God? The Man assures us that unless we change and become like little children, we will not enter the Kingdom of God. Whoever becomes like a child is of the greatest importance in the heavenly reign. *Teach me to be! Get fired up!*

The young man understood, with the wonderment of a child, that all the natural and moral laws had their opposites. The proper use of power in unconditional love will defeat and forgive the misuse of power in the evil, ugly, violent acts of abuse, crucifixion, and torture. *Be positive!*

The young man looked forward to the moment when he would receive a two-handed applause. He would have faith in The Man. He would achieve according to his gifts. *Multitask!*

Bibliography

Bible, the New Jerusalem. Printed in the United States of America: Darton, Longman & Todd, Ltd. and Doubleday & Company, Inc. 1985.

Brown, Dan. *Angels & Demons.* New York: Simon & Schuster, Inc. 2003.

Collins, Francis S. *The Language of God: A Scientist Presents Evidence for Belief.* New York: Simon & Schuster, Inc. 2005.

Drake, Frank. *Is Anyone out There? The Scientific Search for Extraterrestrial Intelligence.* New York: Bantam Doubleday Publishing Group, Inc 1992.

Gregory, David. *A Day with a Perfect Stranger.* WaterBrook Press. Colorado Springs, Colorado. 2006.

Hawking, Steven W. *A Brief History of Time: From the Big Bang to Black Holes.* Bantam Books. New York, New York. 1988.

Hawking, Steven W. *A Brief History of Time: The Updated and Expanded Tenth Anniversary Edition.* Bantam Books. New York, New York. 1996.

Hawking, Steven W. *A Briefer History of Time.* Bantam Books. New York, New York. 2005.

Hawking, Steven W. *A Brief History of Time* The page numbers are from Hawking's *A Brief History of Time: From the Big Bang to Black Holes.* Bantam Books. New York, New York. 1988.

Isaacson, Walter. *Einstein: His Life and Universe*. New York: Simon & Schuster. 2007.

McBride, James J. (1935–present) *A Proposed Biotic System: A Possible Definition and Descriptor of Reality*. Dissertation presented to the graduate faculty of the School of Human Behavior. San Diego: United States International University. 1975.

Meacham, Jon. *American Gospel God, the Founding Fathers*, and the *Making of a Nation*. New York: The Random House Publishing Group, a division of Random House, Inc. 2007.

Molnar, Michael R. *The Star of Bethlehem: The Legacy of the Magi*. New Brunswick. New Jersey and London: Rutgers University Press. 2000.

Parker, Barry. *Chaos in the Cosmos: The Stunning Complexity of the Universe*. New York: Plenum Press, a division of Plenum Publishing Corporation. 1996.

Paul was the apostle to the Gentiles (5–67 AD) *Bible, the New Jerusalem*, "The Introduction of Paul," page 1849.

Prigogine, Ilya (1917–2003). *The End of Certainty: Time, Chaos, and the New Laws of Nature*. New York: A Division of Simon & Schuster Inc. 1997.

Ratzinger, Joseph. Pope Benedict XVI. *Jesus of Nazareth: From the Baptism in the Jordan to the Transfiguration*. New York: The Double Broadway Publishing Group, a division of Random House, Inc. 2007.

Sources

I wrote this book, *The Man and a Boy,* as a father to five, a father-in-law to four, a grandfather to twenty-three, a great-grandfather to seven … and as an uncle and a friend. I am first a husband, and somewhere along my journey, I was a teacher. My goal in this book is to teach about abuse, mathematics, science, and theology. Each of these subjects has a unique set of rules. All subjects have a set of rules. All behaviors come with a set of rules. Regulating and deregulating a set of rules is a choice each of us makes to lead our lives. However, each of us has a responsibility to our planet, and to each other. We will not be abusive by forcing a set of rules on another.

Sources are paramount for this book. These sources—authors, mathematicians, scientists, and theologians—have or had a unique way of presenting their ideas to the world. They have their rules. Their ability to communicate their ideas in their unique fashion is their genius. My meager gift as a husband of fifty-five years, a teacher of forty-two years, and now a novice author is to find a way to present these geniuses to my readers. I have used the words, paraphrased the words and noted the words of these geniuses so full credit is to them.

The bibliography, annotated bibliography, and description honor the genius of each of my cited heroes, idols, and authors. They are colossal in my feelings and thoughts. Their words are prominent for the story in this book. This book is part quotes, part paraphrases, and part generalization of what has tickled me from these geniuses. Your homework as a reader is to learn from as many of these geniuses as you can. I hope they tickle your heart, mind, and soul as they did mine.

I want to give credit when I quote and when I paraphrase their work. I have included authors that have helped my thinking with their ideas and concepts.

Annotated Bibliography
Descriptions

Wikipedia, the Free Encyclopedia is a treasure chest I accessed on the Internet to further my knowledge of the idols. http://en.wikipedia.org source

Archimedes (287–212 BC)
  http://en.wikipedia.org/wiki/
  Special:Search?search=Archimedes.+287-212+B.C.+&go=Go

  He is generally considered the greatest mathematicians of antiquity, and one of the greatest of all time. He was a physicist, an engineer, an inventor, and an astronomer. He influences my thinking greatly. From his genius comes the development of technological tools. I must have told his story about the bathtub and density a thousand times. "Eureka, I found it."

The Bible has many different versions. I have two. I find the New Jerusalem Bible the easiest to read, with the best footnotes. I find all versions of the Bible a passionate love story of God.

Brown, Dan. *Angels & Demons.*

  From Wikipedia, the Free Encyclopedia.
  http://en.wikipedia.org/w/index.php?title=Special%3ASearch
  &search=Dan+Brown++&ns0=1&fulltext=Search

  He is an American author of thriller fiction, best known for the 2003 best-selling novel *The Da Vinci Code*, and the above 2000 best-selling novel *Angels & Demons*. He grabs your attention with his fiction.
  I read his works with suspended disbelief. I believed what he said about the set of rules of the Catholic Church, but in the end, I examined the set of rules for myself.

Buddha, Siddhārtha Gautama (563–483 BC)

Wikipedia, the Free Encyclopedia. http://en.wikipedia.org/wiki/Buddha

Buddha was a spiritual teacher from ancient India and the founder of Buddhism He is generally recognized by Buddhists as the Supreme *Buddha* The time of his birth and death are uncertain. He is the Enlightened One. He said, "Each of us is a God. Each of us knows all. We need only open our minds to hear our own wisdom." I seek enlightenment, so I followed the advice of Buddha by opening my mind to the wisdom that comes from a greater god.

Collins, Francis S. *The Language of God: A Scientist Presents Evidence for Belief*

From Wikipedia, the Free Encyclopedia
http://en.wikipedia.org/wiki/Francis_S._Collins

Francis S. Collins, MD, PhD, is one of the world's leading scientists. He is an American physician-geneticist, noted for his landmark discoveries of disease genes, and his leadership of the Human Genome Project (HGP). He was director of the National Human Genome Research Institute (NHGRI).

Dr. Collins has described his parents as "only nominally Christian," and by graduate school, he considered himself an atheist. However, dealing with dying patients led him to question his religious views, and he investigated various faiths. He became an evangelical Christian after observing the faith of his critically ill patients and reading *Mere Christianity* by C. S. Lewis.

In his 2006 book, Collins considers scientific discoveries an "opportunity to worship." Collins examines and subsequently rejects creationism and intelligent design. The most accurate system is theistic evolution (TE) with the following premises: The universe came into being out of nothingness, approximately fourteen billion years ago. Despite massive improbabilities, the properties of the universe appear to have been precisely tuned for life. While the precise mechanism of the origin of life on Earth remains unknown, once life arose, the process of evolution and natural selection permitted the development of biological diversity and complexity over long periods. Once evolution got under way, no special supernatural intervention was required.

Humans are part of this process, sharing a common ancestor with the great apes. However, humans are also unique in ways that defy evolutionary explanation and point to our spiritual nature. This includes the existence of the moral law (the knowledge of right and wrong) and the search for God that characterizes all human cultures throughout history.

I used his words and quoted extensively. During forty-two years of teaching many subjects, six of those years included biology. I understand the words and the set of rules for biology; however, I could not find any words better than those of Dr. Collins. His work is phenomenal.

Drake, Frank. *Is Anyone out There?*

From Wikipedia, the Free Encyclopedia
http://en.wikipedia.org/wiki/Frank_Drake

In 1960, Drake, a radio astronomer, conducted the first radio search for extraterrestrial intelligence, known as Project Ozma. While he was sifting through the noise and looking at a handful of stars, no evidence for ET signals emerged. Drake commonly regards "contact" as inevitable in the coming years, in the form of a radio or light signal. In 1961, he developed his famous equation.

I added his equation to my book because I think God is open-minded and thinks outside the box. He would not restrict his love to one planet.

Feynman, Richard Phillip (1918–1988)

From Wikipedia, the Free Encyclopedia
http://en.wikipedia.org/wiki/Richard Feynman

Richard Phillips Feynman was an American physicist known for the path integral formulation of quantum mechanics, the physics of the super fluidity of super cooled liquid helium, as well as work in particle physics. For his contributions to the development of quantum electrodynamics, Feynman was a joint recipient of the Nobel Prize in Physics in 1965. His diagrams of particle interactions are called perturbation theory, later becoming known as Feynman diagrams.

During his lifetime, Feynman made physics popular in his books and lectures, notably a 1959 talk called "There's Plenty of Room at the Bottom" and *The Feynman Lectures on Physics.* Feynman is also known for his semiautobiographical books: *Surely You're Joking, Mr. Feynman!* and *What Do You Care What Other People Think?*

He is also my idol. I attended a lecture of his at Stanford University in 1964. From that moment, I tried to emulate him in being his student and in my teaching of physics. He, more than anyone, helped me to see the world from different frames of references, and to understand the sets of rules in those frames of reference.

Gauss, Johan Carl Friedrich (1777–1855)

From Wikipedia, the Free Encyclopedia
http://en.wikipedia.org/wiki/Johann_Carl_Friedrich_Gauss

Johan Carl Friedrich Gauss was a German mathematician and scientist who contributed significantly to many fields, including number theory, statistics, differential geometry, electrostatics, astronomy, and optics. Gauss was a child prodigy. There are many anecdotes pertaining to his precocity while a toddler, and he made his first groundbreaking mathematical discoveries while still a teenager.

I add this anecdote: If Gauss, at ten years old, could solve a math problem in five minutes, and I, at twenty years old, could solve the same problem in twenty minutes, then using the inverse square law, I could say I was one sixty-fourth as smart as my hero Gauss. In all my years of teaching, I made it a point to teach each of my students as if he or she were Gauss.

Gregory, David, *A Day with a Perfect Stranger.*

I read his books after I had my epiphany about The Man and a boy. The idea of Jesus, as a modern man, talking to human beings about their problems, was a neat concept. David Gregory helped me to expand on the concepts of love, agape, and unconditional love.

Hawking, Steven W. *A Brief History of Time*

From Wikipedia, the Free Encyclopedia
http://en.wikipedia.org/wiki/Steven_Hawking

It was only necessary for him to know that something could be done, and that he could do it without looking to see how other people did it. He didn't have very many books, and he didn't take notes. Of course, his mind was completely different from those of his contemporaries.

Hawking's principal fields of research are theoretical cosmology and quantum gravity. In the late 1960s, he and his Cambridge friend and colleague, Roger Penrose, applied a new, complex mathematical model they had created from Albert Einstein's general theory of relativity. This led, in 1970, to Hawking proving the first of many singularity theorems; such theorems provide a set of sufficient conditions for the existence of a singularity in space-time. This work showed that far from being mathematical curiosities that appear only in special cases, singularities are a fairly generic feature of general relativity.

He supplied a mathematical proof, along with others, namely that any black hole is fully described by the three properties: mass, angular momentum, and electric fields. Hawking also suggested that upon analysis of gamma ray emissions, after the big bang, primordial or mini black holes were formed. With others, he proposed the four laws of black hole mechanics, drawing an analogy with thermodynamics. In 1974, he calculated that black holes should thermally create and emit subatomic particles, known today as Hawking radiation, until they exhaust their energy and evaporate.

Hawking had earlier speculated that the singularity at the center of a black hole could form a bridge to a "baby universe," into which the lost information could pass; such theories have been very popular in science fiction. However, according to Hawking's new idea, black holes eventually transmit, in a garbled form, information about all matter they swallow.

This man is brilliant! While all of us have one kind of handicap or another, amyotrophic lateral sclerosis, or ALS, disables Hawking. This condition is known in the United States as Lou Gehrig's disease. To overcome or work through a handicap is the subject of my book. Steven Hawking exemplifies what my book is trying to teach.

Isaacson, Walter. *Einstein: His Life and Universe.*

From Wikipedia, the Free Encyclopedia
http://en.wikipedia.org/wiki/Walter_Isaacson

The question of scientific determinism gave rise to questions about Einstein's position on theological determinism, and whether or not he believed in a God. In 1929, Einstein told Rabbi Herbert S. Goldstein, "I believe in Spinoza's God, who reveals Himself in the lawful harmony of the world, not in a God Who concerns Himself with the fate and the doings of mankind."

In a 1950 letter to M. Berkowitz, Einstein stated, "My position concerning God is that of an agnostic. I am convinced that a vivid consciousness of the primary importance of moral principles for the betterment and ennoblement of life does not need the idea of a law-giver, especially a law-giver who works on the basis of reward and punishment."

Einstein also stated: "I have repeatedly said that in my opinion the idea of a personal God is a childlike one. You may call me an agnostic, but I do not share the crusading spirit of the professional atheist."

He developed the laws of special relativity in 1905, with two axioms: (1) All inertia frames of reference are equivalent; and (2) The speed of light is constant, as proved by Maxwell's equations. General relativity came years later.

Einstein not only helps me understand physics and the universe, but he also helps me understand the philosophy and the set of rules for each science, theology, and most other subjects.

Maxwell, James Clerk (1831–1879)

From Wikipedia, the Free Encyclopedia
http://en.wikipedia.org/wiki/James_Clerk_Maxwell

James Clerk Maxwell was a Scottish mathematician and theoretical physicist. His most significant achievement was the development of the classical electromagnetic theory, synthesizing all previous unrelated observations, experiments and equations of electricity, magnetism, and even optics into a consistent theory. His set of equations describes electricity, magnetism, and even light. The equations are all manifestations of the same phenomenon: the electromagnetic field. From that moment on, all other classical laws or equations of these disciplines became simplified cases of Maxwell's equations. His work in electromagnetism has been called the "second great unification in physics," after the first unification carried out by Newton.

I thoroughly enjoy learning about his works in physics. You don't know physics unless you thoroughly know Newton and Maxwell. Whatever influence he had with his friend Lewis Carroll (Charles Dodson) in the writings of *Alice* has had a great influence over my life. I cherish the great allegories of physics in the stories of Alice. The Cheshire Cat is a metaphor for Maxwell's equations.

McBride, James J. (1935–present)

This is my doctoral dissertation on four-dimensional systems. It gives me the ability to analyze systems for values, a set of rules, logic, and experiences as a function of time.

Meacham, Jon. *American Gospel.* A fantastic read for me. This was an education for me about the truth of the separation of church and state.

Molnar, Michael R. *The Star of Bethlehem* This book, for me, was the final piece to the puzzle. It made whole the knowledge I gained over the years when I presented The Star of Bethlehem in a junior college planetarium.

Parker, Barry. *Chaos in the Cosmos.* I learned an awful lot about chaos theory from this author and his book.

Pascal, Blaise (1623–1662)

From Wikipedia, the Free Encyclopedia
http://en.wikipedia.org/wiki/Blaise_Pascal

Pascal was a French mathematician, physicist, and religious philosopher. A child prodigy, he was educated by his father. Pascal's earliest work was in the natural and applied science. Pascal also wrote in defense of the scientific method. Blaise Pascal's wager called "hedging your bets," presented in Dialogue Sixteen, was a fun idea.

Paul was the apostle to the Gentiles (5–67 AD) *Bible, the New Jerusalem.*, "The Introduction of Paul," page 1849.

From Wikipedia, the Free Encyclopedia
http://en.wikipedia.org/wiki/Paul_the_Apostle

Paul, along with Saint Peter and James the Just, was the most notable of early Christian missionaries. Unlike the Twelve Apostles, there is no indication that Paul ever met Jesus before the latter's Crucifixion.

From my Bible, The Introduction of Paul, page 1849.

Paul was born in Tarsus in Cilicia in about 10 AD. He was a Jew born to the tribe of Benjamin. He was a Roman Citizen. He was educated as a Pharisee embracing the law. His genius was more intellectual than imaginative. His enthusiasm was with the rigid logic of law. He was a Jew with a strong Hellenistic Greek background. In 34 AD, he had a vision of the risen Jesus. God's grace worked through him.

He had a great dedication to an ideal. He had a single-minded determination. He was a hard worker who refused to compromise. He worked through his exhaustion. He suffered through ridicule, poverty, and danger of death. He was sensitive, trusting, and furious when needed. He got upset with vanity and was ironical with superficiality. He could be tender, fatherly, and extremely indignant against seducers of his converts. He was conciliatory with Peter. He died in Rome.

Poincaré, Jules Henri (1854–1912)

From Wikipedia, the free encyclopedia
http://en.wikipedia.org/wiki/Jules_Poincare
As a mathematician and physicist, he made many original fundamental contributions to pure and applied mathematics, mathematical physics, and celestial mechanics. In his research on the three-body problem, Poincaré became the first person to discover a chaotic deterministic system, which laid the foundations of modern chaos theory. He is considered one of the founders of the field of topology. I include Poincare for helping me understand chaos theory.

Prigogine, Ilya

From Wikipedia, the Free Encyclopedia
http://en.wikipedia.org/wiki/Ilya_Prigogine

In his book *The End of Certainty*, Nobel Prize winner Prigogine contends that determinism is no longer a viable scientific belief. The more we know about our universe, the more difficult it becomes to believe in determinism. This is a major departure from the approaches of Newton, Einstein, and Schroedinger, all of whom expressed their theories in terms of deterministic equations. According to Prigogine, determinism loses its explanatory power in the face of irreversibility and instability.

Prigogine traces the dispute over determinism back to Darwin, whose attempt to explain individual variability according to evolving populations inspired Ludwig Boltzmann to explain the behavior of gases in terms of populations of particles rather than individual particles. This led to the field of statistical mechanics and the realization that gases undergo irreversible processes. In deterministic physics, all processes are time reversible, meaning that they can proceed backward as well as forward through time.

As Prigogine explains, determinism is fundamentally a denial of the arrow of time. With no arrow of time, there is no longer a privileged moment known as the "present," which follows a determined past and precedes an undetermined future. All of time is simply given, with the future as determined as the past. With irreversibility, the arrow of time is reintroduced to physics. Prigogine notes numerous examples of irreversibility, including diffusion, radioactive decay, solar radiation, weather, and the emergence and evolution of life. Like weather systems, organisms are unstable systems existing far from thermodynamic equilibrium. Instability resists standard deterministic explanation. Instead, due to sensitivity to initial conditions, unstable systems can only be explained statistically—that is, in terms of probability.

Prigogine asserts that Newtonian physics has now been extended three times, first with the use of the wave function in quantum mechanics, then with the introduction of space-time in general relativity, and finally, with the recognition of indeterminism in the study of unstable systems.

He asked questions! What are the roots of time? Did time start with the big bang? I worked hard learning his ideas. I hope I did him justice by quoting his ideas.

Ratzinger, Joseph

From Wikipedia, the Free Encyclopedia
http://en.wikipedia.org/wiki/Joseph_Ratzinger_as_Prefect_of_the_Congregation_for_the_Doctrine_of_the_Faith

Benedict XVI is a respected Roman Catholic theologian and a

prolific best-selling author, a defender of traditional Catholic doctrine and values. He served as a professor at various German universities and was a theological consultant at the Second Vatican Council before becoming archbishop of Munich and Freising, and later a cardinal. At the time of his election as Pope, he had been prefect of the Congregation for the Doctrine of the Faith, and he was dean of the College of Cardinals.

For this reason, he proclaims relativism's denial of objective truth—and more particularly, the denial of moral truths—as the central problem of the twenty-first century. He teaches the importance of the Catholic Church for humanity to contemplate God's salvific love. He has reaffirmed the "importance of prayer in the face of the activism and the growing secularism of many Christians engaged in charitable work."

I enjoyed his point of view. He clarified the man, Jesus, for me. Looking at Jesus from many frames of reference and from a different set of rules can only open one's mind, heart, and soul. This book helped me to understand and feel love, agape, altruism, and unconditional love.

Riemann, Georg Friedrich (1826–1866)

From Wikipedia, the Free Encyclopedia
http://en.wikipedia.org/wiki/Georg_Friedrich_Bernhard_Riemann

Georg Friedrich Riemann was a German mathematician who made important contributions to analysis and differential geometry, some of them paving the way for the later development of general relativity.
In 1853, Gauss asked his student Riemann to prepare a lecture on the foundations of geometry. Over many months, Riemann developed his theory of higher dimensions. When he finally delivered his lecture at Göttingen in 1854, the mathematical public received it with enthusiasm, and it is one of the most

important works in geometry. "On the Hypotheses Which Underlie Geometry" was published in 1868.
I learned non-Euclidean geometry by studying his works.

Acknowledgments

This book would not have been possible without the extraordinary support of a number of people. I begin with my wife, Janet. She is my rock.

I want to express my appreciation to three neighbors: Mary Anne Baker, Tom Christian, and Bob Jackson. We share books, ideas and similar philosophies. They were helpful at the beginning stage of the editing process. I am so grateful for Bob's expertise in marketing, Tom's expertise in law, and Maryanne's general knowledge in publishing. They were insightful and meticulous in correcting details and helping the flow of the text.

I especially want to thank Dr. Margaret Wright, who has used her expertise as an English teacher to correct and edit everything of importance that I ever wrote. She is a fellow teacher, colleague, and advisor in our teachers' association in Coronado; we are still friends after retiring.

Endnotes

1 Bible, the New Jerusalem. Printed in the United States of America: Darton, Longman & Todd, Ltd. and Doubleday & Company, Inc. 1985. Matthew 18:5,6

2 Ibid. Matthew 18:1,5

3 Ibid. Matthew 11:28–30

4 Title of picture by Greg Olsen, Same picture on front cover

5 Bible, op. cit., Matthew 5:1–16

6 Ibid. Matthew 5:17–18

7 Ibid. Matthew 18:1–9

8 Ibid. John 1:1–3

9 Collins, Francis S. *The Language of God: A Scientist Presents Evidence for Belief* New York: Simon & Schuster, Inc. 2005. p.74 Constants can be found in a scientific dictionary.

10 Bible, op. cit., John 1:4–5

11 Ibid. Genesis 11:1–9

12 Ibid. John 1:9–12

13 Hawking, Steven W. *A Brief History of Time: From the Big Bang to Black Holes*. Bantam Books. New York, New York. 1988.
A Brief History of Time: The Updated and Expanded Tenth Anniversary Edition. Bantam Books. New York, New York. 1996.
A Briefer History of Time. Bantam Books. New York, New York. 2005.
The page numbers are from Hawking's *A Brief History of Time: The Updated and Expanded Tenth Anniversary Edition* pp. 149–152, 155

14 Prigogine, Ilya (1917–2003). *The End of Certainty: Time, Chaos, and the New Laws of Nature*. New York: A Division of Simon & Schuster Inc. 1997.
Scientist agree on the concept of *The Arrow of Time* pp. 1–2, 19, 73, 102.

15 Bible, op. cit., Matthew 7:15–16

16 Ibid. Genesis 1:14-19

17 Prigogine, op. cit., *The Arrow of Time.* pp. 1–2, 19, 73, 102

18 Ibid., *The Arrow of Time.* pp. 1–2, 19, 73, 102

19 Ibid., pp. 4–6

20 Ibid., pp. 4–6

21 Ibid., pp. 28–31; Hawking, op. cit., pp. 9, 46, 49–53, 119–122, 125–127; Parker, Barry. *Chaos in the Cosmos: The Stunning Complexity of the Universe.* New York: Plenum Press, a division of Plenum Publishing Corporation. 1996.

22 Pascal, Blaise (1623–1662) His wager called "hedging your bets" presented in the encyclopedia.

23 Isaacson, Walter. *Einstein: His Life and Universe.* New York: Simon & Schuster. 2007. pp. 316, 317, 320–21, 323–25, 331–334, 340, 345, 347, 349, 455

24 Bible, op. cit., Genesis 1:20–31

25 Collins, op. cit., p.24 Bible, op. cit., Matthew 6:25–34

26 Hawking, op. cit., pp. 49, 51–53, 119–122, 125–127

27 Bible, op. cit., Matthew 8:26

28 Bible, op. cit., Matthew 5:1–10

29 Prigogine, op. cit., pp. 28–31 Parker, op. cit., p 84

30 Isaacson (Einstein), op. cit., pp. 138, 139

31 Isaacson (Einstein), op. cit., pp. 118, 122

32 Maxwell, James Clerk (1831–1879), a Scottish mathematician and theoretical physicist.

33 Isaacson (Einstein and Maxwell), op. cit., pp. 91–92

34 Constants are found in any science dictionary or on the internet.

35 Prigogine, op. cit., pp.30–31, 36

36 Prigogine, op. cit., pp. 172–173, 175, 179

37 Bible, op. cit., Deuteronomy 32:39

38 Humenik, John M., publisher and editor Arizona Daily Star article, 2007.

39 DNA–deoxyribonucleic acid is found in any science dictionary or on the internet.

40 Prigogine, op. cit., pp. 6, 163–164, 172–175

41 Hawking, op. cit., pp. 9, 46, 49, 119–122

42 Hawking, op. cit., pp. 12–14, 72–75, 160, 167, 171–172

43 Hawking, op. cit., pp. 18–23

44 Hawking, op. cit., pp. 125, 136, 144–145, 149–153, 155–156

45 Hawking, op. cit., See bibliography for his history.

46 Prigogine, op. cit., pp. 15–16, 179, Cosmology

47 Hawking, op. cit., pp. 87, 120, 128–131, Cosmology

48 Hawking, op. cit., pp. Hawking radiation, pp. 131, 145, 174, 176

49 Hawking, op. cit., pp. 63, 81, 83–84

50 Hawking, op. cit., 11, 30–35

51 Hawking, op. cit., Anthropic principle, pp. 137, 142, 155, 180

52 Bible, op. cit., Psalm 8

53 Bible, op. cit., Psalm 19

54 Hawking, op. cit., pp. 49–50

55 Hawking, op. cit., forces pp. 70–76

56 Bible, op. cit., Romans 1:18

57 Bible, op. cit., Romans 2:1

58 Bible, op. cit., Saint Paul the Apostle

59 Bible, op. cit., Paul's Letters to the Romans and Galatians

60 Bible, op. cit., Psalm 19:11–14

61 Bible, op. cit., Psalm 27

62 Bible, op. cit., Psalm 27:10

63 Collins, op. cit., p. 66

64 Hawking, op. cit., pp.49, 53 Collins, op. cit., pp. 62–65

65 Hawking, op. cit., pp. 121–123 Collins, op. cit., pp. 67–68

66 Hawking, op. cit., pp. 124–125 Collins, op. cit., pp. 69–70

67 Hawking, op. cit., pp. 125–126 Collins, op. cit., pp. 71–78

68 Collins, op. cit., p. 69

69 Collins, op. cit., pp. 71–72

70 Collins, op. cit., pp. 72–73

71 Collins, op. cit., pp. 73–74

72 Collins, op. cit., p. 69

73 Bible, op. cit., p. 1157 Prophets

74 Pascal, op. cit., Pascal's wager

75 Isaacson, Einstein, op. cit., pp.90–91

76 Isaacson, Einstein, op. cit., pp.320–325

77 Isaacson, Einstein, op. cit., pp.331–332

78 Collins, op. cit., pp. 78–80

79 Drake, Frank. *Is Anyone out There? The Scientific Search for Extraterrestrial Intelligence.* New York: Bantam Doubleday Publishing Group, Inc 1992.   The Drake equation (cc) = 1st x 2nd x 3rd x 4th x 5th x 6th x 7th

80 Prigogine, op. cit., p. 4

81 Prigogine, op. cit., p. 4

82 Prigogine, op. cit., pp. 153–154

83 Prigogine, op. cit., p. 155

84 Hawking, op. cit., pp. 9, 46, 49–53, 119–122, 125–127

85 Prigogine, op. cit., p. 3–5

86 Prigogine, op. cit., pp. 1–7

87 Prigogine, op. cit., pp.18–19

88 Prigogine, op. cit., pp. 26–27

89 Prigogine, op. cit., pp. 183–184

90 Prigogine, op. cit., pp. 177–182

91 Prigogine, op. cit., pp. 1–7

92 Bible, op. cit., Matthew 12:50. Brother and Sister, The New Jerusalem Bible

93 Bible, op. cit., Interpretation of Galatians according to an encyclical by Pope Pius XII on literary Forms: "The interpreter of a (literary form) must endeavor very carefully, overlooking no light derived from recent research to determine the personal traits and background of the sacred writer, the age in which he lived, the oral or written sources which he used, and his ways of expressing himself... It is absolutely necessary for the interpreter to return in spirit to the remote ages to use the resources of history, archaeology, and the other sciences, to determine what precisely were the so called literary forms which the writers of the time customarily used."

94 Ibid., Interpretation of Romans

95 Gregory, David. *A Day with a Perfect Stranger.* WaterBrook Press. Colorado Springs, Colorado. 2006.

96 Molnar, Michael R. *The Star of Bethlehem: The Legacy of the Magi.* New Brunswick. New Jersey. And London: Rutgers University Press.2000

97 Bible, op. cit., Matthew 2:1,2

98 Molnar, Michael R. *The Star of Bethlehem: The Legacy of the Magi.*

New Brunswick. New Jersey, London: Rutgers University Press. 2000

99 Collins, op. cit., The title of his book: *The Language of God: A Scientist Presents Evidence for Belief*

100 Ibid. pp. 5–6

101 Ibid. pp. 25–28, 165

102 Ibid. pp. 27–28, 217

103 Ibid. pp. 45–47

104 Ibid. pp. 42–45

105 Ibid. pp. 29, 51

106 Ibid. pp. 80–83

107 Ibid. pp. 80–83

108 Ibid. pp. 80–83

109 Ibid. pp. 80–83

110 Ibid. pp. 88–90

111 Ibid. pp. 90–93

112 Ibid. pp. 91–93

113 Ibid. pp. 91–93

114 Ibid. pp. 91–93

115 Ibid. pp. 91–93

116 Ibid. pp. 97

117 Ibid. pp. 101

118 Ibid. pp. 101

119 Ibid. pp. 102

120 Ibid. pp. 102

121 Ibid. pp. 103

122 Ibid. pp. 104

123 Ibid. pp. 107

124 Ibid. pp. 101–107

125 Ibid. pp. 104

126 Ibid. pp. 104

127 Ibid. pp. 106

128 Ibid. pp. 107.

129 Ibid. pp. 107

130 Ibid. pp. 124

131 Ibid. pp. 125

132 Ibid. pp. 126

133 Ibid. pp. 140

134 Ibid. pp. 140

135 Ibid. pp. 141

136 Ibid. pp. 161

137 Ibid. pp. 172–174

138 Ibid. pp. 185–195

139 Ibid. pp. 199–206

140 Ibid. pp. 200

141 Ibid. pp. 200–201

142 Ibid. pp. 204–205

143 Ibid. pp. 205–228

144 Ibid. pp. 228

145 Bible, op. cit.,1 Cor 13:13

146 Parker, Barry. *Chaos in the Cosmos: The Stunning Complexity of the Universe.* New York: Plenum Press, a division of Plenum Publishing Corporation. 1996.pp. 4–7

147 Ibid. pp. 7–11

148 Parker, op. cit., pp. 31–39

149 Parker, op. cit., pp.41–43

150 Parker, op. cit., pp.48–51

151 Parker, op. cit., pp.52–58

152 Parker, op. cit., pp.59–62

153 Parker, op. cit., pp.63–66

154 Parker, op. cit., pp.67–74

155 Parker, op. cit., pp.74–82

156 Gregory, David. *A Day with a Perfect Stranger.* WaterBrook Press. Colorado Springs, Colorado. 2006. pp. 62, 76–78

157 Ibid. pp. 77, 84–87

158 Ibid. pp. 82–83, 89

159 Ibid. pp. 53–55

160 Ibid. pp. 55, 59, 76, 78, 79

161 Bible, op. cit., Matthew 11:28–30